Beautifully Said

QUOTES BY REMARKABLE WOMEN AND GIRLS
DESIGNED TO MAKE YOU THINK

Quotabelle®

ROCK
POINT

For fellow citeseers, quote enthusiasts,
and lovers of true stories ~
an invitation to wander, wonder,
and find what speaks to you

Inspiring | Educating | Creating | Entertaining

Brimming with creative inspiration, how-to projects, and useful information to enrich your everyday life, Quarto Knows is a favorite destination for those pursuing their interests and passions. Visit our site and dig deeper with our books into your area of interest: Quarto Creates, Quarto Cooks, Quarto Homes, Quarto Lives, Quarto Drives, Quarto Explores, Quarto Gifts, or Quarto Kids.

First published in 2017 by Rock Point, an imprint of The Quarto Group, 142 West 36th Street, 4th Floor New York, NY 10018 USA
T (212) 779-4972 **F** (212) 779-6058 **www.QuartoKnows.com**

14

ISBN: 978-1-63106-310-7

Quotabelle: Pauline Weger and Alicia Williamson
Editorial Director: Rage Kindelsperger
Managing Editor: Erin Canning
Editorial Project Manager: Chris Krovatin
Art Director and Cover Design: Merideth Harte
Interior Design: Tara Long

Printed in China 1010022020

CONTENTS

THE QUOTEUR LIST

QUOTEUR™/KWŌ TƏR/ NOUN | A PERSON WHO ORIGINATES
A COLLECTION OF WORDS WORTH SHARING

THE POWER OF A FEW SHORT WORDS

There are quotes meant for rousing and some carefully chosen to be eloquent or strong. Quotations can fill a void when otherwise there might be simply no words. Or light up classroom discussions, provide writing prompts, or kick off exams. They provoke thoughts, challenging or new. They set the tone for a team, or give way to reflection. Long inked in journals and books, quotations can be brimming with wisdom or simply state the obvious. Words can become signature statements, creatively capturing the essence of a person. Some make you wonder. Others reveal possibilities. They often leave an imprint or perhaps preserve a legacy. Delivered in just the right place and at just the right time, you'll hear audible "ahs" and see the nodding of heads and sometimes waves of laughter. When carefully chosen and thoughtfully shared, quotes are as good as gifts. Rousing. Provocative. Eloquent. Wonder-inducing. Touching. Glib. Poignant. On point. Quite simply, quotes are gems.

BUT, WHERE ARE THE SMART, INSIGHTFUL, FUNNY THINGS SHE HAS SAID?

Of the millions of quotes shared every day, a mere 14 percent are by women or girls. And, most of those are from the same few names. What started as a casual observation while writing a book led to research, with hands-on help from a legion of equally intrigued friends, students, recent grads, and teachers. It evolved into a female founder (baby boomer) teaming with a like-minded university educator (millennial), who both asked, "Isn't there a more modern, engaging way to discover the ideas and stories of women and girls?"

This is the era of social entrepreneurship. When we see a problem, we're inspired to create a solution. So, we're fixing the quote supply problem. Our ultimate goal: surfacing ideas that spark thinking while ensuring even more female role models emerge. We're delighted to present our first print collection of quotations and stories from remarkable women and girls; designed to make you think.

A PLAYGROUND OF IDEAS.

Every quote in this collection leads to hundreds more online—all researched and sourced at Quotabelle.com. What makes us uniquely us: you'll also find true stories there; the lives behind the lines.

We're adding missing voices back into history and ensuring modern-day thinkers aren't overlooked going forward. Enjoy discovering our gallery of sheroes. Inventors. Entrepreneurs. Athletes. Activists. Artists. Entertainers. Technologists. Scientists. Coaches. Leaders. And more.

Cheers,

PAULINE & ALICIA

SHE BELIEVES

DOROTHY DAY

{1897–1980}

JOURNALIST · FOUNDER OF THE CATHOLIC WORKER MOVEMENT ·
CANDIDATE FOR SAINTHOOD

A Bohemian intellectual in her youth, this socialist journalist became a model Catholic convert. Dorothy put her newfound faith into practice through social justice activism as a voice of compassion and mercy during the Great Depression and beyond. Besides advocating for equality and pacifism, she was the founding editor of the *Catholic Worker*, a popular newspaper that launched a movement to bring dignity to everyday people. Farming communes, charitable centers, and homeless shelters were founded around the country according to Dorothy's openhearted principle—accepting all in need for as long as help is needed.

"Food for the body
is not enough.
There must be food
for the soul."

DOROTHY DAY
SOCIAL REFORMER

HILDEGARD OF BINGEN

{1098-1179}

SPIRITUAL ADVISOR TO POPES AND KINGS · COMPOSER ·
DOCTOR OF THE CHURCH

This Benedictine nun from medieval Europe was a true renaissance woman . . .
two centuries before the Renaissance. Known as Sybil of the Rhine, Hildegard
was famous for her divine visions of humans connected to the earth as living sparks
of God's love. Nine hundred years later, her soaring chants still grace public radio
and her texts on holistic medicine inspire modern-day healers.

"Humanity, take a good look at yourself. Inside, you've got heaven and earth, and all of creation. You're a world— everything is hidden in you."

HILDEGARD OF BINGEN
SAINT

ANN LEE

{1736-1784}

TEXTILE WORKER · CHRISTIAN LEADER · SPIRITUAL MOTHER AND HEALER

This illiterate Englishwoman rose above religious persecution and an unhappy arranged marriage to become the prophet behind one of history's longest-running utopian communities. Her spin-off from a sect in England became a small community of immigrants, called Shakers, based in rural New York. Shaker villages spread from New England to Ohio and Kentucky, drawing thousands of members and surviving for more than two hundred years (in spite of the chastity requirement). Mother Ann's other guiding principles? Secluded communal living, gender and racial equality, and the duty to work. Today, examples of Shaker workmanship exist in furniture, textiles, and crafts, sought after for their elegant simplicity and utility.

"Put your hands to work, and your hearts to God."

ANN LEE
FOUNDER OF THE SHAKERS

MARIANNE WILLIAMSON

{BORN 1952}

CABARET SINGER • NEW AGE RELIGIOUS LEADER • SELF-HELP GURU

Marianne was raised in a Jewish family but found her calling outside of organized religion. As a best-selling author and fiery orator, she's one of the most influential voices in contemporary spirituality. Central to her message: act out your beliefs in the world—don't just "dwell in light," but "be a light." Marianne has practiced what she preaches by establishing Project Angel Food, cofounding the Peace Alliance, and running for political office. This particular quotation is part of a rousing call that's often misattributed to the late Nelson Mandela.

"Our deepest fear is not that we are inadequate, it is that we are powerful beyond measure."

MARIANNE WILLIAMSON
SPIRITUAL TEACHER

SHARON SALZBERG

{BORN 1952}

LOVING-KINDNESS ADVOCATE · MEDITATION TEACHER · RETREAT PIONEER

This New York City native's troubled childhood left her feeling lost and undeserving of love. On a spiritual quest to India, Sharon found healing and a calling in Buddhist meditation. Today, the ancient practice has worked its way into mainstream society, introduced everywhere from elementary schools to corporate offices, helping people focus and reduce stress. As cofounder of a meditation retreat center, Sharon has played a vital role in making tradition speak to twenty-first-century life. She inspires worldwide practitioners to seek deeper awareness through mindful living.

"Faith is a willingness to take the next step, to see the unknown as an adventure, to launch a journey."

SHARON SALZBERG
BUDDHIST LEADER

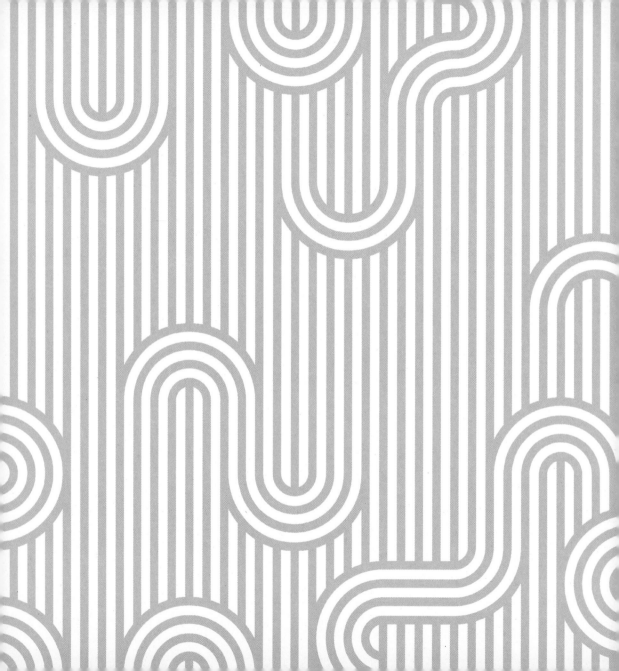

SHE BUILDS

MADAM C.J. WALKER

{1867–1919}

DAUGHTER OF SLAVES • BEAUTY CULTURIST • PHILANTHROPIST

This young widow went from dollar-a-day washerwoman to the United States' first female self-made millionaire. Madam C.J. built a world-famous cosmetics brand from $1.50 in start-up capital and door-to-door sales of her own hair-care formulas. By the time she retired, the enterprising inventor had her own factory, beauty school, and sales force of several thousand women, whom she encouraged to follow her lead by empowering themselves through financial independence. Today, an upswell of support for Madam C.J.'s legacy means that you can once again find her beauty culture brand on retailers' shelves.

"Don't sit down and wait
for opportunities to come . . .
get up and make them!"

MADAM C.J. WALKER
COSMETICS ENTREPRENEUR

ZAHA HADID

{1950-2016}

ARTIST · MATHEMATICIAN · STARCHITECT

Dubbed the Queen of the Curve, Iraqi-born Zaha rose to the top of a male-dominated field with innovative designs that combined ultra-modern engineering with stunning organic—and sometimes gravity-defying—lines. The founder of her own London-based firm, Zaha claims international credits such as a museum tucked into an Alpine cliff, a Chinese opera house inspired by the riverbank it overlooks, and a radically reimagined auto plant in Germany. She was known for her courage and conviction, and for being the first woman to win a Pritzker (considered the Nobel Prize of architecture). Her sudden passing raises the question: Why aren't there more Zahas?

"There are 360 degrees,
so why stick to one?"

ZAHA HADID
ARCHITECT

SHEILA JOHNSON
{BORN 1949}

CONCERT VIOLINIST • TV NETWORK PIONEER • HOSPITALITY INDUSTRY INNOVATOR

Formerly a music teacher, Sheila cofounded the first African-American cable network, then became the first African-American female billionaire when she sold Black Entertainment Television in 2002. Sheila has continued to follow her instincts ever since, with bold, new business and philanthropic ventures. For her "third act," she decided to try her hand as a hotel magnate in the five-star hospitality industry. Sheila stuck with her vision for ten years, finally locking in the approvals to debut a stylish resort in Virginia's horse country. The seemingly tireless maker is also a groundbreaking film producer, arts patron, photographer, scarf designer, and owner of a professional women's basketball team.

"Once you've explored
all your options,
you have to know when
to let it go."

SHEILA JOHNSON
SERIAL ENTREPRENEUR

LINDA ALVARADO

{BORN 1951}

CONTRACTOR • RESTAURANT INVESTOR • PRO BASEBALL TEAM OWNER

This athletic girl who grew up in a poor Albuquerque family with five brothers has thrived in two male-dominated fields—construction and pro sports. After her business plan for a construction startup was rejected six times, she parlayed a small loan from her parents and successes on small projects into game-changing contracts, building everything from arenas to high-rises. Linda's investment in the Colorado Rockies made her the first female and first Hispanic owner in Major League Baseball. She's proof that brains and guts form a solid foundation to build upon—one that's helped her break the "concrete ceiling."

"You are never going to get to second base if you keep your foot safely on first."

LINDA ALVARADO
CONSTRUCTION EXEC

DEBBIE STERLING

{BORN 1983}

ENGINEER • STEM CHAMPION • CHANGE-MAKER

As one of the few female engineering grads in her class, Debbie set out to transform the demographics of a field that's still 86 percent male. Using a clever viral video to fuel a successful crowdfunding campaign, she launched GoldieBlox, an educational toy company that pairs colorful building sets with stories starring adventurous kid inventors. Besides taking on the traditional toy-store "pink aisle," Debbie's making sure that our girls develop the confidence and skills to literally "build the future."

"Failure breeds invention."

DEBBIE STERLING
TOYMAKER

SHE CHAMPIONS

EMMA WATSON
{BORN 1990}

MODEL • UNITED NATIONS GOODWILL AMBASSADOR • ACTOR

Emma was learning the ropes at a performing arts school when the she was tapped to play a starring role in the Harry Potter film series . . . one of the most successful film franchises of all time. After growing up on-screen as Harry's brainy BFF Hermione Granger, Emma signed on to a courageous new role as a goodwill ambassador with UN Women. She's using her celebrity to engage millennials in cross-gender feminism as the global spokesperson for the UN's #HeForShe campaign. Today, you can find Emma sitting down for one-on-ones with fellow activists, leading a solidarity-building book club, and doing post-grad work in gender studies.

"I don't want other people
to decide who I am.
I want to decide that for myself."

EMMA WATSON
"HEFORSHE" CHAMPION

ELIZABETH CADY STANTON
{1815-1902}

ABOLITIONIST • SENECA FALLS ORGANIZER • SUFFRAGIST

Besides co-organizing the United States' first women's rights conference—the historic Seneca Falls Convention—Elizabeth drafted its iconic set of resolutions, The Declaration of Sentiments. Though confined by her domestic duties as a mother of seven, her influence expanded when she met Susan B. Anthony. The two cofounded the Women's National Loyal League during the Civil War and the National Woman's Suffrage Association afterward. Elizabeth would write fiery speeches, while Susan would deliver the "thunderbolts." A successful lobbyist for legal reforms to marriage laws and the first woman to run for Congress, Elizabeth never became a "face" of the suffragist movement because of her controversial stances on religion and reproductive rights. Today, she's celebrated as a progressive thinker who was well ahead of her time.

"The best protector any woman can have, one that will serve her at all times and in all places, is courage."

ELIZABETH CADY STANTON
WOMEN'S RIGHTS ADVOCATE

ROSA PARKS

{1913-2005}

SEAMSTRESS • PROTEST CATALYST • ADVOCATE FOR URBAN YOUTH

Most people know Rosa as the mild-mannered Alabama seamstress who happened to change the world on her way home from work. Trained by the NAACP in nonviolent resistance, Rosa was ready to make a brave statement when the opportunity presented itself. Her moment came when she refused to give up her seat in the black section of the bus to a white man who couldn't find an open seat in the white section at the front. Her arrest sparked the successful Montgomery Bus Boycott. This defining moment in the Civil Rights movement is memorialized with a permanently seated statue of Rosa at the U.S. Capitol in Washington, D.C.

"The only tired I was,
was tired of giving in."

ROSA PARKS
CIVIL RIGHTS ICON

GLORIA STEINEM
{BORN 1934}

THE FACE OF SECOND-WAVE FEMINISM • "HOPE-AHOLIC" • PUBLISHER

After an itinerant childhood, Gloria was left to care for her mentally ill mother when her father abandoned them. She made her own way as a gutsy New York City journalist, evolving into a "galvanizer" who helped launch a new wave of feminism. Since the 1960s, Gloria has been "waging peace" to win tangible gains for gender equality, using mainstream media and politics to channel her message. Now in her eighties, the cofounder of *Ms. Magazine* and Take Our Daughters to Work Day is still writing, speaking, and stirring things up. She continues to remind us that "not everyone has to live the same way."

"The future depends entirely on what each of us does every day. After all, a movement is only people moving."

GLORIA STEINEM
FEMINIST

SHIRIN EBADI
{BORN 1947}

JUDGE • LAW PROFESSOR • NOBEL PEACE PRIZE LAUREATE

In 1969, Shirin became Iran's first female judge. After the 1979 revolution, she was forced to leave the bench to become a clerk in the court she used to oversee. Instead of accepting the demotion, Shirin fought for her lawyer's license so that she could take on high-profile, pro bono cases and champion the rights of women, children, refugees, and political dissidents. Today, the cofounder of the Defenders of Human Rights Center is forced to speak from exile in the UK. A face of the Muslim feminist movement, she sees humanitarian work as a "form of worship."

"When you strongly believe
in a principle or a cause,
courage to pursue it
will follow."

SHIRIN EBADI
HUMAN RIGHTS ACTIVIST

ERTHARIN COUSIN
{BORN 1957}

LAWYER • NONPROFIT AND CORPORATE EXEC • AMBASSADOR

When appointed the top exec of the United Nations' World Food Programme, Ertharin tasked herself with an audacious goal—to end hunger during her lifetime. At the helm of the largest humanitarian organization, this visionary director is well on her way. Besides feeding ninety-seven million people a year, Ertharin and her team roll out programs that anticipate catastrophic disasters—like those brought on by climate change—and then proactively provide resources such as drought-resistant seeds. She's passionate about helping at-risk populations withstand crises and boost resilience in order to make hunger history.

"Let us be the crazy ones,
the ambitious ones,
the ones who see beyond
the limits of today."

ERTHARIN COUSIN
GLOBAL HUNGER RELIEF LEADER

SHE COACHES

EMILY POST

{1872-1960}

COLUMNIST • AUTHOR • FOUNDER OF A (STILL-THRIVING) ETIQUETTE INSTITUTE

This heiress built an empire on etiquette—which, according to Emily, isn't simply good manners but also good ethics. Her expertise on the subject was born from experience. The socialite found herself embroiled in a high-profile scandal when her messy divorce proceedings made headlines. A lifelong writer, Emily decided to put her talents toward helping others navigate the tricky business of everyday life. While much has changed in the world of formal social protocol, Emily's tenets of gracious living remain guideposts.

"Only the very small mind hesitates to say 'I don't know.'"

EMILY POST
ETIQUETTE EXPERT

JULIA CHILD
{1912–2004}

WWII INTELLIGENCE OFFICER • COOKBOOK AUTHOR • FOODIE ICON

The woman who failed her first exam at Paris's celebrated Le Cordon Bleu went on to be the most famous proponent of French cuisine outside France. Having felt failure herself, the dauntless Julia was eager to take the "bugaboo" out of Continental cooking for the rest of us through her wildly popular cookbooks and her own TV show. Audiences tuned in for decades to see Julia's practical instructions and infectious enthusiasm brought to everything from pâté to soufflé. Her kitchen—meticulously recreated from her Cambridge, Massachusetts, home—is a must-see for museumgoers visiting the Smithsonian in Washington, D.C.

> "The pleasures of the table, and of life, are infinite— *toujours bon appétit!*"

JULIA CHILD
CHEF

JOYCE BROTHERS

{1927-2013}

ADVICE COLUMNIST • BROADCASTING PERSONALITY • THE FACE OF PSYCHOLOGY

Dr. Joyce enjoyed her first taste of the limelight when she took home the top prize on a TV quiz show for her uncanny knowledge of boxing trivia. But this doctor's biggest claim to fame was making the human psyche accessible as the first mainstream media psychologist. Over her storied career, she dished much-needed counsel via TV talk shows, radio programs, best-selling books, and more than fifty years of daily advice columns.

"Cherish everything in your day that contributes to happiness: spending a special moment with a child, drinking a cup of your favorite coffee, joking with a co-worker, saving a rosebush from destruction. Happiness hides in life's small details. If you're not looking, it becomes invisible."

JOYCE BROTHERS
PSYCHOLOGIST

MÁRTA KÁROLYI
{BORN 1942}

CHOREOGRAPHER • GYM FOUNDER • TEAM LEADER FOR USA GYMNASTICS

This former gymnast first won international recognition as part of the wife-husband coaching team that led Nadia Comăneci to an all-around gold plus the first perfect 10 in Olympic gymnastics history. Soon after, Márta defected from Romania to the United States, where she and her husband Béla set up an elite gym on a Texas ranch. Known as Team USA's "technician" for her eagle-eyed and stone-faced approach, Márta and her coaching brilliance continued to shine through even after Béla stepped down. The centralized national training system she implemented saw Team USA win five consecutive international championships, and helped the Final Five (the gymnastics team named in honor of Márta's coaching finale) dominate at the 2016 Rio Olympics.

"I don't know if I'd say I'm strict. I'd rather say that I'm very consistent with my expectations."

MÁRTA KÁROLYI
GYMNASTICS COACH

MARIE KONDO

{BORN 1985}

ATTENDANT MAIDEN AT A SHINTO SHRINE • AUTHOR • TIDIEST WOMAN IN THE WORLD

This Japanese organization expert grew up poring over lifestyle magazines, and at nineteen turned her passion into a career as a decluttering guru, clearing people's homes, lives, and minds. Raised in a culture where it's not uncommon to think of objects as having souls, Marie developed a trademark tidying method based on one simple question: "Does it spark joy?" (Hint: Keep those things that do; respectfully thank and discard those things that don't.) Her theories have made such a splash that her name has become a verb: KonMari!

"The space in which we live should be for the person we are becoming now, not for the person we were in the past."

MARIE KONDO
TIDYING PRO

SHE COMPETES

MIA HAMM
{BORN 1972}

TEEN SOCCER PRODIGY • THREE-TIME ESPY WINNER •
COFOUNDER OF FIRST FEMALE PROFESSIONAL SOCCER LEAGUE

At fifteen years old, this soccer all-star was the youngest person to make the national team. Mia won two Olympic golds and two World Cup titles during her seventeen-year tenure on Team USA. Along the way, she earned a serious fan following for women's soccer, using her high-profile successes to help cofound the first female professional league. Generally considered the best all-around player in the sport, Mia, now retired, is focused on creating opportunities for young female athletes to find their passion and discover the confidence and connections that come with the thrill.

"Somewhere behind the athlete you've become and the hours of practice and the coaches who have pushed you is a little girl who fell in love with the game and never looked back . . . play for her."

MIA HAMM
SOCCER PLAYER

ELLEN MACARTHUR

{BORN 1976}

SOLO YACHTSWOMAN • HONORARY DAME • FOUNDATION FOUNDER

At age twenty-four, Ellen turned heads with her second-place finish in one of the world's most challenging races, a solo offshore sailing trek around the globe. Three years later, she became the fastest person to circumnavigate the earth single-handedly, completing the twenty-six-thousand mile route in just under seventy-two days. Now, Dame Ellen has retired from racing to do service work. Her charitable trust takes young cancer patients sailing because rebuilding self-esteem impacts recovery. Her foundation is mapping ways to rejigger our economy toward a "regenerative, circular" model inspired by nature.

"When you're a child, anything and everything is possible. The challenge, so often, is hanging on to that as we grow up."

ELLEN MACARTHUR
YACHTSWOMAN

SERENA WILLIAMS
{BORN 1981}

FASHION DESIGNER • ACTOR •
THE WORLD'S HIGHEST-EARNING FEMALE ATHLETE

This comeback queen has overcome injuries and illness, criticism and skepticism to work her way up to the world's number one tennis player six different times over the course of her two-decade career. Coached and homeschooled by her parents alongside her sister Venus, Serena went pro at age fourteen, and won the U.S. Open in 1999. Today, she's the oldest woman ever to hold tennis's top spot, with a record-tying twenty-two Grand Slam singles titles (plus sixteen doubles titles and four Olympic golds). Many consider this power player, known for her statement-making style, to be the Greatest Of All Time when it comes to the courts. Watch one of her 128-mile-per-hour serves whiz by, and you'll know why.

"It's really about taking
one moment at a time
and trying to master
those moments."

SERENA WILLIAMS
TENNIS PLAYER

JAMIE ANDERSON

{BORN 1990}

SLOPESTYLE CHAMPION SNOWBOARDER • NATURALIST • ZEN ATHLETE

Tahoe-born Jamie took up snowboarding at age nine and was winning medals at the X Games by her early teens. Known for her infectious positivity, Jamie keeps herself centered during competitions with pre-game meditation and incense. It's a ritual that helped her bring home gold in the first-ever Olympic slopestyle event at the 2014 Winter Games. Today, this air-catcher is continuing to push the limits of a male-dominated sport. Besides bringing home multiple awards as an action sport hero, she collaborates with the other women of slopestyle to show just how far the sport has come.

"I'd rather be inspired
by my competition
than be jealous."

JAMIE ANDERSON
SNOWBOARDER

ASHIMA SHIRAISHI
{BORN 2001}

Ashima took her first climb at age six, when she couldn't resist scaling a rock in New York's Central Park. At fourteen, she was dubbed one of the all-time greatest rock climbers, crushing gravity-defying routes up cliffs from Chile to Japan with astonishing agility and grace. The youngest person to achieve a V15 ascent, this bouldering phenom is making history by tackling the world's most daring and difficult climbs with wise-beyond-her-years determination.

"Climbing isn't easy . . .
It's repetitive falling.
But once you stand up,
you're that much closer
to the top."

ASHIMA SHIRAISHI
ROCK CLIMBER

SHE DESIGNS

COCO CHANEL
{1883–1971}

ORPHAN · CABARET SINGER · HAUTE-COUTURE LEGEND

The illegitimate daughter of a laundrywoman and a clothes peddler, Coco was taught to sew by nuns in the French abbey orphanage where she spent six years. She rolled that skill into a revolutionary career that ushered in a new century of high style, overturning fussy, ornate, corset- and bustle-bound fashions with modern, less-is-more elegance. While her background stirs up controversies that have inspired books and films, her signature style goes unquestioned. With credits that include the little black dress, pencil skirt, feminine suits, strings of pearls, and the world's most popular perfume, Coco's classics remain today's chic staples.

"One cannot be forever innovating.
I want to create classics."

COCO CHANEL
FASHION DESIGNER

DOROTHY DRAPER

{1889-1969}

NORM-BUCKING DEBUTANTE • AGENCY FOUNDER • DESIGN INDUSTRY PIONEER

This high-society trendsetter translated her lavish sense of style into a thriving business . . . and then transformed interior design into an industry. Dorothy's bold decor—from striking checkerboard floors to cabbage rose chintz—turned staid neighborhoods and hotels into en-vogue hot spots flooded with color. At the time considered America's most influential tastemaker, she shared her know-how in popular DIY guides that helped Americans design their way out of the "Drab Age," and convinced tentative housewives to embrace the first rule of decorating: courage. Today, Dorothy's trusted collaborators continue her legacy.

"I firmly believe that
nothing contributes so much
to the beauty of this world
as color."

DOROTHY DRAPER
INTERIOR DESIGNER

GEORGIA O'KEEFFE

{1887–1986}

MIDWEST FARM GIRL · TEACHER · "MOTHER OF MODERNISM"

She's one of the world's best-loved artists, but there was a time when the unconventional Georgia gave up her charcoals out of frustration with the realist bent of the art world. Coaxed back by brilliant educators, the pioneering painter left her mark on modern art, from New York to New Mexico. Georgia's captivating close-ups ask us to re-see everyday objects and spark intimate wonder at the natural world. The continuing appreciation of her original perspective made for a recent art-world milestone—a white flower she painted in 1931 sold at auction for $44.4 million, a record for any female artist.

"Take time to look . . ."

GEORGIA O'KEEFFE
PAINTER

JULIANE BLASI
{BORN 1977}

CAR LOVER • AVID TRAVELER • TRANSPORTATION IMAGINEER

Only two years after scoring her dream job at BMW, the German-born Juliane became the first woman in the luxe car company's history to win one of their internal contests (nicknamed "bakeoffs"). The prize? To design their next roadster. The super sleek and powerful 2009 Z4, BMW's first hardtop convertible, was an instant hit on the roads. The refined interior of Juliane's imagination-capturing concept car was crafted by her female design partner, Nadya Arnaout.

"For the designer
it is existentially important to
get different effects, to travel,
to see other things.
Creativity needs width."

JULIANE BLASI
CAR DESIGNER

MONIQUE PÉAN
{BORN 1981}

INVESTMENT BANKER · SOCIAL ENTREPRENEUR · JURASSIC JEWELER

Monique was working on Wall Street when her teen sister's death in a car crash made her radically rethink her future. Leaving behind a high-flying career in finance, she found a way to combine her passions for travel, design, and philanthropy by bringing eco-chic to the fine jewelry industry. Each of her stunning handmade collections is inspired by the indigenous cultures, traditional artisans, and locally sourced materials (think: meteors, dinosaur fossils, and woolly mammoth tusks!) from remote places where Monique has trekked. Her work has not only left the fashion industry greener, but it has also set the standard for giving with philanthropic initiatives that benefit developing countries.

"It is important to recognize that everyone can make a little bit of difference, and that, in aggregate, our individual daily efforts add up."

MONIQUE PÉAN
ECO-JEWELRY DESIGNER

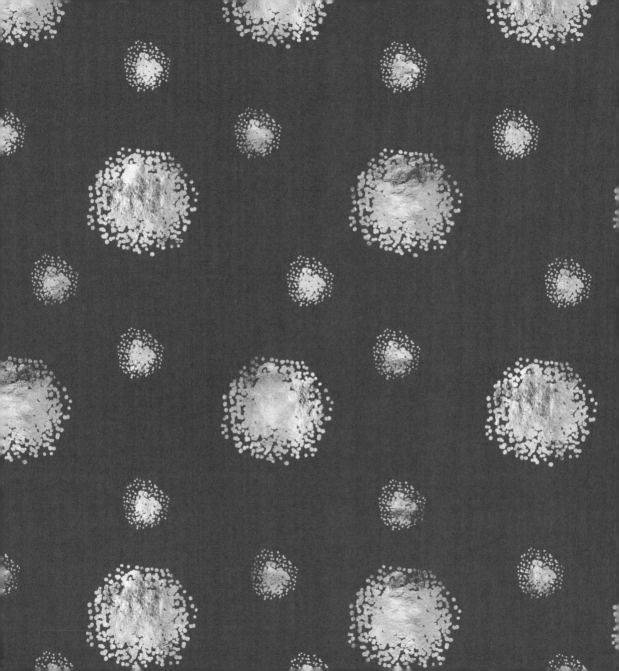

SHE DISCOVERS

MARIA MITCHELL

{1818–1889}

Maria (pronounced muh-RYE-uh) was an amateur stargazer who worked and studied her way to become the United States' first female pro astronomer. Her father taught her the ropes of the telescope on a deck atop their Nantucket house, where she would "sweep the heavens." Maria's 1847 discovery of a comet earned her a gold medal from the King of Denmark and recognition as the first woman elected to the American Academy of Arts and Sciences. Hired as Vassar College's very first professor, Maria lived in the campus observatory built specially for her and regularly hosted much-loved Dome Parties for her appreciative students.

"The more we see, the more
we are capable of seeing."

MARIA MITCHELL
ASTRONOMER

ZORA NEALE HURSTON

{1891–1960}

FOLKLORIST • CULTURE EXPLORER • NOVELIST

Zora went from being one of the Harlem Renaissance's most celebrated and prolific authors to a penniless unknown during her lifetime. She spent her final days in a welfare home and was laid to rest in an unmarked grave. It wasn't until her 1970s revival by then up-and-coming author Alice Walker that Zora's lyrical writing became rightfully established as required reading and her magnum opus *Their Eyes Were Watching God* was officially designated a Great American Novel. Trained in field research, Zora treated her literary work as a "spyglass of anthropology," chronicling Southern black folk cultures—from her native Florida to the Caribbean and Central America—that might otherwise have gone unrecorded.

"No matter how far
a person can go
the horizon is still
way beyond you."

ZORA NEALE HURSTON
ANTHROPOLOGIST

SYLVIA EARLE
{BORN 1935}

OCEANOGRAPHER • SEA EXPLORER • HERO FOR THE PLANET

Dubbed Her Deepness, Sylvia has logged more than seven thousand hours underwater. She has led more than a hundred expeditions to explore the vast and largely unknown reaches of our oceans. Sylvia's love for exploring came early in her childhood, when her family moved to the Florida coast. She followed that kidlike wonder to become the first female head of the U.S. National Oceanic and Atmospheric Association, a pioneer of marine engineering and a National Geographic explorer-in-residence. Today, the bold oceanographer is on a mission to create protected marine zones called "Hope Spots" to save and restore the vital "blue heart of the planet."

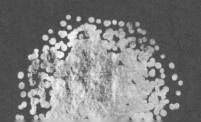

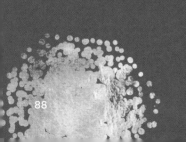

"The best scientists and explorers have the attributes of kids. They ask questions and have a sense of wonder. They have curiosity. Who, what, where, why, when, and *how*!"

SYLVIA EARLE
MARINE BIOLOGIST

LESLIE GORDON

{BORN 1964}

MEDICAL DOCTOR • SAM'S MOM • FOUNDATION COFOUNDER

When this MD found out that her twenty-two-month-old son Sam had progeria, she made it her mission to find a cure for the fatal condition that causes rapid, premature aging. Since the disease claims most victims by age fourteen, Leslie's work was a race against time. She and her husband (a fellow pediatrician) created the Progeria Research Foundation, laying out the path to identify the gene that causes the rare disease and discover a possible treatment within a decade. Teenaged Sam—who shared his hopes and positive outlook in speeches, articles, and a stirring documentary—raised awareness by putting a heroic face on the cause. While a cure wasn't found in time to save Sam, his remarkable life inspires Leslie and the team to be unwavering in the fight.

"What do you do when there's nowhere to turn?
You drive straight ahead."

LESLIE GORDON
MEDICAL RESEARCHER

SARAH PARCAK

{BORN 1979}

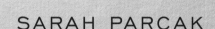

EGYPTOLOGIST • PROFESSOR • SPACE ARCHAEOLOGIST

"If Indiana Jones and Google Earth had a love child . . . " That's how Sarah describes her work of tracking down important archaeology from above, via satellite imaging. Her novel twenty-first-century methods garnered a $1 million prize from TED, an organization of innovators on a mission to find ideas worth spreading. Sarah is using that grant to create a platform for recruiting citizen scientists to not just locate ancient ruins but also protect the world's historic sites from looting and wartime devastation. It'll be a vital new tool for this archaeologist, whose research has proved that there are treasures worth studying practically everywhere!

"We have survived as a species for over 100 thousand years. What's amazing to me as an archeologist is the more and more I study, the more I realize: We are resilient. We are creative. We are brilliant. And this is what makes us human. And that has not changed since we've been human."

SARAH PARCAK
ARCHAEOLOGIST

SHE ENTERTAINS

MAE WEST

{1893–1980}

SCREENWRITER · COMEDIAN · THE QUEEN OF CAMP

Mae defied the Hollywood bias toward bright, young things to become a late-breaking superstar of the silver screen. With a vaudeville background and serious comedic chops, this sassy leading lady not only acted the parts, she wrote them, too. Mae was constantly at odds with Hollywood censors, but she never shied away from controversy, or from delivering up one of her trademark double entendres. A muse to many, Mae was courted by the Beatles to appear on the album cover of *Sgt. Pepper's Lonely Hearts Club Band*, and artist Salvador Dalí was so enchanted that he fashioned a luscious surrealistic sofa inspired by her lips.

"I've found
too much of a good thing
can be wonderful."

MAE WEST
ACTOR

ANNETTE KELLERMAN

{1886–1975}

CLIFF DIVER · SILENT FILM STAR · HEALTH AND FITNESS ENTREPRENEUR

Annette discovered her love of all things aquatic when she took up swimming in sea baths as part of a rehab regimen for her childhood polio. As a long-distance swimmer and later a movie star, she helped redefine the feminine ideal—from ornately concealed, corset-cinched frailty to barely covered, robust strength. Known as the Original Mermaid, Annette popularized swimming as a sport through books and films. But her most significant contribution may well be the one-piece swimsuit. Even though Annette's form-fitting alternative initially got her arrested on obscenity charges, it quickly became the norm.

"I learn much from people
in the way they meet
the unknown of life."

ANNETTE KELLERMAN
SWIMMER

ELLA FITZGERALD

{1917–1996}

ORPHAN · BEBOP PIONEER · THE QUEEN OF JAZZ

A last-minute bout of stage fright made seventeen-year-old Ella switch her act from dancing to singing at the Apollo Theater's Amateur Night. It was a decision that not only saw her take home the top prize but also launched a legendary sixty-year vocal career. She showed off her extraordinary three-octave range and signature scat style in more than two thousand recorded songs that breathed new life into old standards. With loads of celebrity fans, this First Lady of Song broke barriers as a fourteen-time Grammy winner (including one for Lifetime Achievement) who performed on the world's biggest stages. She remains one of history's most celebrated singers.

"The only thing
better than singing
is more singing."

ELLA FITZGERALD
SINGER

GEENA DAVIS
{BORN 1956}

OSCAR WINNER • FILM FESTIVAL FOUNDER • GENDER-EQUALITY CHAMPION

This leading lady built her acting career playing strong, quirky, authentic women who determined their own destiny. When interesting scripts became scarce, she took a real-world leading role as a feminist change-maker. In 2007, she founded the Geena Davis Institute on Gender in Media to offer solutions to imbalances in the global entertainment industry, from what we see on-screen to behind the scenes. Geena's groundbreaking studies show through hard numbers how the media perpetuates stereotypes. But the optimistic activist believes the industry can crack the problems it has created. Today, she balances her time between acting roles and off-screen advocacy to "change what the future looks like." Her Institute's motto has become: If she can see it, she can be it.™

"Here's what I always say:
If they can see it,
they can be it."

GEENA DAVIS
ACTOR

SHONDA RHIMES

{BORN 1970}

AUTHOR • TV EXECUTIVE PRODUCER • "SAY YES" ADVOCATE

The first African-American woman to have a top-ten network TV show, Shonda has become a celebrity writer and producer. Her hit medical dramas and legal thrillers share a common thread—strong female leads. Besides being riveting entertainment, Shonda's work is helping to make television reflect real-world diversity while ensuring characters are real-world complex. Along the way, she's had personal "aha" moments about having a dream job that doesn't allow ample time for dreaming. Now, she embraces "goofing off" to keep the wonder alive.

"Work doesn't work without play."

SHONDA RHIMES
SCREENWRITER

SHE EXPLORES

NELLIE BLY

{1864-1922}

ASPIRING WRITER · GROUNDBREAKING NEWSPAPER REPORTER · WORLD-RECORD-SETTING TRAVELER

This ambitious undercover reporter (whose real name was Elizabeth Cochran Seaman) got herself committed to the "madhouse" so she could pen an exposé on mental institutions. Nellie's writing provoked shock, then reform. It was a bold move that ensured she'd never be assigned another "fluff" piece. After a few years as a star correspondent for Joseph Pulitzer's *New York World*, she pitched her next big story— a solo trip around the world. The much-publicized journey put Nellie on the map as the first woman and fastest person to circle the globe, clocking the whopping 24,899 miles by train and steamship in just over seventy-two days.

"I need a vacation; why not take a trip around the world?"

NELLIE BLY
INVESTIGATIVE REPORTER

MARGARET "MOLLY" TOBIN BROWN
{1867–1932}

SHOPGIRL • SOCIALITE • PHILANTHROPIST

The daughter of Irish immigrants, Margaret became a cosmopolitan traveler and the toast of Denver society after her husband struck it rich in the mining industry. Already a darling of the press as a fresh and frank member of the nouveau riche, she became an international sensation as the most famous survivor of one of the twentieth century's most notorious tragedies—the sinking of the *Titanic* ocean liner off the coast of Newfoundland. Mythologized as the Unsinkable Molly Brown in a hit movie and musical of the same name, the real-life Margaret was equally impressive. She was a fearless adventurer who used her celebrity to accomplish progressive reforms, pioneer the juvenile court system, and run for U.S. Senate before women could even vote.

"I am a daughter of adventure. This means I never experience a dull moment and must be prepared for any eventuality."

MARGARET "MOLLY" TOBIN BROWN
TITANIC SURVIVOR

MAE JEMISON
{BORN 1956}

PHYSICIAN · ARTS ENTHUSIAST · SPACE EXPLORER

This young Trekkie grew up with cosmic ambitions and went on to make
her sky-high dreams come true as the first African-American woman in space . . .
not to mention the first real-life astronaut to appear in a *Star Trek* series. After
serving as a Peace Corps medical officer in Liberia and Sierra Leone, Mae was selected
from among two thousand applicants to be a mission specialist aboard NASA's
Endeavor shuttle. She conducted life-science experiments and bone-cell research
while making 127 orbits around the Earth. Today, this former physician, professor,
and founder of two tech companies is only accelerating from rocket ships to
starships as the principal of an organization that's leading the way
to a future that includes travel to and from the stars.

"I had to learn very early not to limit myself due to others' limited imaginations. I have learned these days never to limit anyone else due to my own limited imagination."

MAE JEMISON
ASTRONAUT

ALISON LEVINE
{BORN 1966}

POLAR EXPLORER • DOCUMENTARY PRODUCER • LEADERSHIP COACH

In spite of a dangerous childhood heart condition, Alison became a world-class adventurer. While captaining the first American Woman's Everest Expedition, an incoming storm left her crew a mere two hundred feet shy of the top. On her second attempt, Alison reached the summit, and made history as one of the few to have climbed the highest peak on each continent. Among her takeaways for leaders and teams: improvisation often trumps planning when conditions are in flux.

"Sometimes you have to go backwards in order to eventually get where you want to be."

ALISON LEVINE
MOUNTAIN CLIMBER

LÉA BRASSY

{BORN 1985}

SAILOR • TRAVELING NURSE • BLOGGER

Since being gifted a surfboard as a young teen, Léa has trekked to remote parts of the globe, catching waves and cherishing nature from Iceland to French Polynesia. Early successes in competitions earned her big-name sponsorships. But she left the championship circuit in her wake to become a modern-day nomad who calls a van or boat her home. Through blogs and films, Léa and her equally adventurous boyfriend are chronicling their simple, sustainable lifestyle rooted in chasing passions.

"Simplicity is key to freedom."

LÉA BRASSY
SURFER

SHE GIVES

OPRAH WINFREY
{BORN 1954}

TALK SHOW LEGEND • MEDIA NETWORK FOUNDER • BIG- AND SMALL-SCREEN PRODUCER

A self-made billionaire, Oprah has become one of the world's most powerful people from a career based on being herself and giving back. From the highest-ranked talk show of all time to books, magazines, seminars, and her own network, Oprah's empire is built on helping people overcome past struggles to live their best lives. She also does that with a global record of philanthropy that spans everything from disaster relief to education for unprivileged students of promise to passionate support for the preservation of African-American history.

"Discover who you are, and use who you are in service to the world."

OPRAH WINFREY
PHILANTHROPIST

SOPHIA SMITH

{1796–1870}

MILD-MANNERED REBEL • DEVOUT CHRISTIAN • EDUCATION TRAILBLAZER

Sophia's affluent but frugal New England farming family didn't believe in women's education. But when she became sole heir of the Smith fortune, she decided to put her money where her heart was and fund the formation of an all-female college. Established in 1871, Smith College still ranks amongst the nation's elite higher education institutions. Among its notable alums: Julia Child, Nancy Reagan, Madeleine L'Engle, Gloria Steinem, and Yolanda King. Take it from Sophia, the faithful philanthropist: "Charity is nothing unless it proceeds from the heart."

"Goodness
has more weight
than talents."

SOPHIA SMITH
UNIVERSITY FOUNDER

AUDREY HEPBURN

{1929–1993}

CHORUS GIRL • HOLLYWOOD ICON • CHILDREN'S RIGHTS CHAMPION

She won an Academy Award and Golden Globe for her very first leading role as the heart-winning royal ingénue of *Roman Holiday*. By the end of her captivating career, this dancer-turned-actor had the coveted grand slam of show biz: an E.G.O.T. (Emmy, Grammy, Oscar, and Tony). Today, Audrey remains synonymous with classic cinema and chic style. Behind her big sunglasses and signature look was an elegant spirit. A beneficiary of relief herself while growing up during WWII in Nazi-occupied Netherlands, Audrey identified with the millions of children whose lives she touched. In 1988, she signed on for a "second career" as a goodwill ambassador with the children's rights organization UNICEF.

"Is there anything more important than a child? Is there another time in your life when love, care, tenderness, food, education, are more important than in childhood?"

AUDREY HEPBURN
HUMANITARIAN

ANNE FRANK
{1929–1945}

DIARIST • DREAMER • HOLOCAUST VICTIM

When Anne's Jewish family was forced into hiding during WWII, the bright young girl kept a journal of her experience. After nearly two years living with seven others in an Amsterdam attic, the fifteen-year-old was captured by Nazis. She died six months later in a concentration camp. But her writings survived, as did her short stories and fairy tales that she envisioned would one day become a "proper" book. So astonishingly full of compassion and hope, Anne and her diary were gifts to the world. Her diary has become required reading, as a moving testament to what humanity lost and how the human spirit can endure.

"Give and give again.
Keep hoping, keep trying,
keep giving!
People who give will
never be poor!"

ANNE FRANK
WRITER

MELINDA GATES
{BORN 1964}

COMPUTER SCIENTIST • FOUNDATION COFOUNDER • IMPATIENT OPTIMIST

After a successful career at Microsoft, Melinda left to cofound and cochair the world's largest private foundation. A major driver of global change, The Gates Foundation does important work in health care, education, development, and social policy, relying on technology and crunchy data to guide research, investments, and innovation. But Melinda also relies on listening. Inspired by the countless mothers she has met who want to "bring every good thing" to their children, Melinda has made a point of investing in women. Or, as she puts it, "the people who invest in everyone else."

"Our desire to bring every good thing to our children is a force for good in the world."

MELINDA GATES
PHILANTHROPIST

SHE HEALS

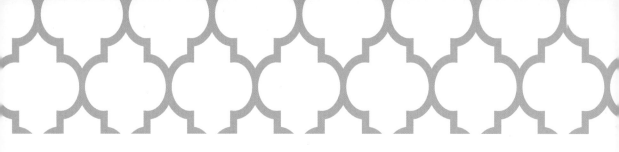

BRENÉ BROWN
{BORN 1965}

SHAME RESEARCHER • DATA-ENTHUSIAST-TURNED-STORYTELLER •
PROFESSOR

This Texas social worker set out to discover the secret to beating vulnerability, but—after years of interviews, analysis, and revelation—she ended up embracing it instead. Why? Because Brené found that acknowledging fears and failures is key to connecting as humans. Today, she's a recovering perfectionist, helping others follow suit through her signature storytelling that's rich with wit and grit yet still rooted in data and research. Brené's popular talks and texts have taught millions how to cope with shame and cultivate courage and worthiness. She's encouraging the world to practice "wholehearted living."

"Every time we choose courage, we make everyone around us a little better and the world a little braver. And our world could stand to be a little kinder and braver."

BRENÉ BROWN
SOCIAL WORKER

FLORENCE NIGHTINGALE
{1820–1910}

STATISTICIAN · REFORMER · THE LADY WITH THE LAMP

Defying pressures to marry well, the British-born Florence followed her calling to Egypt to study as a nurse. In the course of her vividly recorded travels, she had an epiphany in how care should be delivered. Famous for her compassionate treatment of wounded soldiers amidst the brutality of the Crimean War, Florence also improved medicine as a whole. She had a talent for compiling and analyzing data and revealing insights through novel infographics. Her study on how unsanitary conditions spread disease led to major hospital reforms. Even after becoming bedridden, Florence wrote a definitive textbook and founded a school, transforming nursing into a legitimate profession.

"Volumes are now written and spoken upon the effect of the mind upon the body . . . I wish a little more was thought of the effect of the body on the mind."

FLORENCE NIGHTINGALE
NURSE

ELIZABETH BLACKWELL

{1821–1910}

FIRST U.S. FEMALE PHYSICIAN • ABOLITIONIST • EDUCATOR

This music teacher wasn't keen on medicine, but a dying friend's admission that having a female physician would have eased her suffering made Elizabeth determined to become that doctor. When the all-male student body at Geneva Medical School was asked to approve her admittance, all 150 voted "yes" . . . as a joke. She fought her way through the program to become the United States' first female M.D., only to find that her career opportunities were extremely limited. Undaunted, Elizabeth cofounded a New York medical college to enable more women to go into the profession while giving care to the poor. She became a trusted authority on hygiene and childrearing, plus an early promoter of preventive medicine.

"It's not easy to be a pioneer—
but, oh, it is fascinating!"

ELIZABETH BLACKWELL
DOCTOR

ANNA COLEMAN LADD

{1878-1939}

AUTHOR • PORTRAIT ARTIST • RECONSTRUCTION SCULPTOR

Before the days of reconstructive surgery, this sculptor helped disfigured WWI soldiers return home with dignity. The evolving weapons of the era inflicted injuries unlike ever before—with shunned soldiers often referring to themselves as "broken gargoyles." Working from a Red Cross studio in Paris, Anna would meticulously create "portrait masks" using head molds and photographs of the men with facial wounds. The war ultimately influenced Anna's art. The cofounder of the Guild of Boston Artists created sculptures and memorials that spoke to the ravages of battle she encountered firsthand through her studio.

"I am not concerned
with outer obstacles,
only the inner ones."

ANNA COLEMAN LADD
SCULPTOR

MARGARET CHAN
{BORN 1947}

PHYSICIAN • GOVERNMENT OFFICIAL • WHO DIRECTOR-GENERAL

Margaret has spent more than a decade at the helm of the World Health Organization, championing "frugal innovations" to ensure better health care for the world's most vulnerable populations. Her role on the global stage is a far cry from those early days teaching home economics in Hong Kong. Even when physician jobs didn't surface for the newly minted doc, Margaret found her way to public health as a medical officer, serving in the Hong Kong government for twenty-five years before leaving as its first female director of health. Today, she's in charge of a host of public health initiatives, among them defeating diseases and eradicating epidemics from AIDS to Zika, while building modern, reliable health systems essential to peace and progress in our borderless world.

"If we miss the poor,
we miss the point."

MARGARET CHAN
GLOBAL PUBLIC HEALTH LEADER

CLAIRE BERTSCHINGER
{BORN 1953}

AID WORKER · EDUCATOR · LIVE AID INSPIRATION

Claire was serving as a Red Cross nurse in Ethiopia when a TV reporter filmed her undertaking a grim task—choosing which of the hundreds of starving children would receive one of the limited relief meals that day. That image from the frontlines of famine inspired an Irish rock star to launch Live Aid, an entirely new way to spur charitable giving on a global scale. Live Aid brought together big-name celebrities and musicians to record singles and perform at concerts that raised more than $300 million for hunger relief. Declared a Dame in 2010, Claire is now training the next generation of overseas aid workers as a London lecturer on tropical medicine.

"There is nothing sweeter, gentler or softer than water. But water has the power to move mountains."

CLAIRE BERTSCHINGER
NURSE

SHE INSPIRES

MICHELLE OBAMA
{BORN 1964}

LAWYER • "MOM-IN-CHIEF" • CHAMPION OF CHILDREN

Kids are moving and eating healthier lunches. The White House's garden-grown veggies are served at state dinners. Military families are recognized for their sacrifices and treated as true VIPs. Girlpower has gone global through policy and education initiatives. These are a few of Michelle's accomplishments from her tenure at 1600 Pennsylvania Avenue, all while raising two school-age daughters in a loving, levelheaded home. Over eight years as the United States' first African-American first lady, Michelle won hearts and minds the world over with her rousing, heartfelt speeches; classic, all-American style; and genuine, down-to-earth personality. The darling of feminists and traditionalists alike, she's all-in when it comes to her responsibilities as guardian and role model for children everywhere.

"We should always have three friends in our lives: one who walks ahead, who we look up to and follow; one who walks beside us, who is with us every step of our journey; and then, one who we reach back for and bring along after we've cleared the way."

MICHELLE OBAMA
FIRST LADY

HARRIET TUBMAN
{CIRCA 1882–1913}

CONDUCTOR ON THE UNDERGROUND RAILROAD •
UNION SPY • SOON-TO-BE FACE ON THE U.S. $20 BILL

Americans regularly rank Harriet among the nation's greatest heroes. Nicknamed the Moses of Her People, this escaped plantation slave risked her life repeatedly to help free others, conducting nineteen successful trips on the Underground Railroad. During the Civil War, she served as a Union nurse and scout, and led an assault that emancipated 750 slaves. The things she did are captured in the pages of history. The things she said, not so much. Her written words are nearly impossible to come by since Harriet didn't learn to write until late in life. What exists of her spoken words—recorded between the quotation marks—more accurately reflect biographers' biases than her authentic manner. Regardless, her stories and few remaining personal items reveal a faithful fighter for race and gender equality right up to the end.

"I prayed to God to make me strong and able to fight, and that's what I've always prayed for ever since."

HARRIET TUBMAN
FREEDOM FIGHTER

ELEANOR ROOSEVELT

{1884-1962}

SHY ORPHAN • LONGEST-SERVING U.S. FIRST LADY • HUMANITARIAN

Eleanor grew from an awkward, self-conscious girl to one of the world's most admired leaders, transforming the role of first lady from fashionable host to political advocate. So deeply did Eleanor care about issues facing everyday people that she fielded 175,000 letters and gave 75 speeches in each of her twelve years at the White House. Her lifetime output included 27 books, 233 radio shows, 555 articles, and 8,000 columns. But it wasn't until she was named as one of the first delegates to the UN that she coauthored what she considered to be her greatest work: the Universal Declaration of Human Rights.

"You must do
the thing you think
you cannot do."

ELEANOR ROOSEVELT
FIRST LADY

AMELIA EARHART

{1897-1939}

FIRST FEMALE TO FLY SOLO ACROSS THE ATLANTIC •
POPULAR COLUMNIST • AVIATION ICON

When Amelia took flight, she landed an enduring place in the public's imagination. This early aviation pioneer not only broke multiple records, she did so in trendsetting style. Her daring deeds, best-selling books, and luxe fashion lines earned Amelia a worldwide following, advancing the professional prospects of women and her field. The iconic pilot's fame only increased after her specially built Lockheed Electra plane was lost somewhere over the Pacific during her daring last flight—an attempt to circumnavigate the world. We still celebrate Amelia's bold spirit as a woman willing to take risks to make her own and others' big dreams possible.

"The most difficult thing
is the decision to act;
the rest is merely tenacity."

AMELIA EARHART
PILOT

MAYA ANGELOU
{1928-2014}

ABUSE SURVIVOR • RENAISSANCE WOMAN • HUMANITARIAN

Singer. Dancer. Streetcar conductor. These are just a few of the jobs Maya held before she found her calling as a writer. And write she did—everything from best-selling memoirs to poetry, essays to screenplays, cookbooks to greeting cards, all words of wisdom drawn from her turbulent, remarkable life. Maya also became a masterful public speaker, known for delivering soul-stirring speeches that moved people to make changes for themselves and their communities. She remains an inspiration to many, a "phenomenal woman" of unshakable faith.

"Pursue the things
you love doing, and then
do them so well
that people can't
take their eyes off you."

MAYA ANGELOU
WRITER

MALALA YOUSAFZAI
{BORN 1997}

CHILDREN'S RIGHTS CHAMPION • NOBEL PEACE PRIZE LAUREATE •
FEARLESS LEADER

When Malala spoke up for girls' rights to learn, a Taliban gunman attacked her on the bus ride home from school. But the young Pakistani student wasn't silenced by the shooting. Just months after coming out of a coma, Malala proved her voice and message were more powerful than ever with an unforgettable call to action delivered at the United Nations on her sixteenth birthday. The youngest-ever winner of the Nobel Peace Prize has turned a groundswell of support into a global movement aligned to her hope: education for all.

"One child, one teacher, one book and one pen can change the world."

MALALA YOUSAFZAI
EDUCATION ACTIVIST

SHE INVENTS

ROBIN CHASE
{BORN 1958}

ENVIRONMENTALIST • CAR-SHARING INNOVATOR • FOUNDER

With her first start-up, this sustainable transportation innovator helped make the sharing economy the norm. The timing was right for Robin to cofound a company that gave us an alternative to car ownership. Using technology to schedule a vehicle just when you need it, you can count on a car being just a few blocks away in many urban areas and across a host of college campuses. In spite of early bumps along the start-up's road, Zipcar has become the planet's largest car-sharing company. Robin has since launched platforms that allow users to share resources and minimize their carbon footprints while saving money. This entrepreneur is mapping out business models for creating greener futures while changing how the world gets from point A to point B.

"I spend my life building the world I want to live in."

ROBIN CHASE
ENTREPRENEUR

LIZZIE MAGIE

{1866-1948}

STENOGRAPHER • PATENT HOLDER • MONOPOLY CREATOR

An outspoken activist, Lizzie designed educational games to promote progressive causes. Though the Monopoly myth claims it was invented by a man during the Great Depression, it was really Lizzie's brainchild. She had designed The Landlord's Game three decades earlier to teach kids a lesson about how the dice are stacked against everyday people. To her chagrin, her little landlords delighted in playing unscrupulous robber barons. Monopoly became the world's most popular board game, while Lizzie and her social critique were written out of the story.

"I am thankful that I was taught how to think and not what to think."

LIZZIE MAGIE
EDUCATIONAL GAME DESIGNER

GRACE HOPPER

{1906-1992}

PROFESSOR · PROGRAMMING LANGUAGE CREATOR · REAR ADMIRAL

During WWII, this math professor enlisted in the Navy. She soon became the third programmer on the United States' first computer—a massive machine measuring 51 x 8 x 8 feet. Called the Mother of COBOL (the world's most widely used programming language for businesses), Grace specialized in developing English-like coding systems that made computers more programmer- and application-friendly. She also created the first "compiler" to translate between programming languages and coined the fear-inducing computer term "bug" when she discovered an actual moth was the culprit behind a computer failure. After closing out her career by training future techies, Amazing Grace retired from the military at age seventy-nine as a rear admiral and the oldest-serving U.S. naval officer.

"Probably the most dangerous phrase that anyone could use in the world today is that dreadful one: 'But we've always done it that way.'"

GRACE HOPPER
COMPUTER SCIENTIST

TEMPLE GRANDIN

{BORN 1947}

BEST-SELLING AUTHOR • EMMY-NOMINATED MOVIE MUSE • AUTISM ADVOCATE

A leading animal behavior researcher, Temple holds an important niche as an inventor. She designed the more humane livestock handling facilities that corral half the United States' cattle. Her ability to think in pictures is key to how she envisions and invents. And that capacity is directly connected to Temple's autism. Diagnosed at the age of three, she is one of the first public figures to speak openly about life on the spectrum. Her personal story is challenging assumptions about people with autism as a prime example of the strengths of differently abled minds. Temple's work as an autism educator has brought about advances in how society appreciates and taps into the talents of visual thinkers.

"I get satisfaction out of seeing stuff that makes real change in the real world. We need a lot more of that, and a lot less abstract stuff."

TEMPLE GRANDIN
ANIMAL SCIENTIST

DANAE RINGELMANN

{BORN 1978}

DAUGHTER OF SMALL BUSINESS OWNERS • INVESTMENT BANKER • CROWDFUNDING PIONEER

A former Wall Street researcher, Danae left behind the world of high finance to revolutionize the industry by giving everyday people access to dream-realizing capital. Ninety rejections by venture capitalists didn't stop Danae and her cofounders. By the time she turned thirty, they had launched Indiegogo, the world's first and largest crowdfunding platform. Since then, Indiegogo has hosted more than 275,000 campaigns in 224 countries—empowering artists, advocates and entrepreneurs to share their message with supporters to win fans and find backing for ideas, big and small.

"Expect self-doubt when you are building something new and important for the world."

DANAE RINGELMANN
ENTREPRENEUR

SHE LAUGHS

JACKIE "MOMS" MABLEY
{1894–1975}

PERFORMER ON THE CHITLIN' CIRCUIT • TV AND FILM STAR • RECORDING ARTIST

The Original Queen of Comedy, this abused orphan grew up to be so well loved that she was called "the funniest woman in the world" by fans and so loving that she was nicknamed Moms by her fellow performers. Whether on stage or screen, in variety shows or her more than twenty hit comedy albums, Moms always brought down the house with her dowdy, toothless, straight-talking alter ego. Her famously raunchy granny act—never without a "cougar" joke and a song—challenged accepted wisdom and manners of the era. Still going in her seventies, Moms headlined a feature film and became the oldest-living person to have a Top 40 hit for her straight-faced cover of the Civil Rights anthem "Abraham, Martin and John."

"Love is like playing checkers. You have to know which man to move."

JACKIE "MOMS" MABLEY
COMEDIAN

LUCILLE BALL

{1911-1989}

RADIO STAR • SITCOM LEGEND • PRODUCTION COMPANY EXEC

After stints as a failed dancer, model, and anonymous blonde B-movie actor, Lucille tapped her gift for slapstick to go big in comedy. She convinced NBC to pick up her first hit sitcom, *I Love Lucy*, after the act's wild success on the radio and vaudeville stage. When she divorced her costar, she took control of their production company and launched a solo TV show. The bold move won Lucille two Emmys and proved that comedic front women could draw major ratings.

"I get my spontaneous performances out of knowing exactly what I'm supposed to do."

LUCILLE BALL
ACTOR

ROSARIO CASTELLANOS

{1925-1974}

AMBASSADOR • PLAYWRIGHT • FEMINIST THINKER

This writer was raised on her family's ranch in Chiapas before a major Mexican land reform stripped the Castellanos family of their property. An orphaned teen in Mexico City, Rosario found her own way by devoting herself to education, art, and intellectual life. She went from being the author of children's puppet shows to one of the most important literary figures of the century. A revolutionary voice known for championing feminism and indigenous rights, Rosario used humor and satire to critique "macho" culture, giving her readers freedom to question traditions and institutions that seemed intractable.

"We have to laugh. Because laughter, we already know, is the first evidence of freedom."

ROSARIO CASTELLANOS
AUTHOR

"There's power in looking silly and not caring that you do."

AMY POEHLER

{BORN 1971}

COMEDIAN • PRODUCER • SMART GIRLS COFOUNDER

Amy cut her comedic chops by putting herself out there—through gutsy improv and versatile sketch comedy. Since then, she has starred in hit movies and TV series, cohosted fabulously funny awards shows, produced and directed new comedies, and written a best-selling memoir. What makes her a shero across generations of women and men, boys and girls? She's relatable, funny, and comfortably confident. She also shows that teaming with talent makes you better together. Now, as the cofounder of the Smart Girls online community alongside her BFF, Meredith Walker, Amy is helping girls embrace their passions, smarts, and inner goofballs.

"Time spent being carefree is time building an interesting you."

MEREDITH WALKER

{BORN 1970}

STORYTELLER • TALENT EXEC • SMART GIRLS COFOUNDER

Meredith got her start in television working at the award-winning kids' network Nickelodeon, graduating to the role of senior segment producer for *Nick News*. She met her bestie Amy while heading up the talent department at *Saturday Night Live*. Together, they launched Amy Poehler's Smart Girls—an online initiative to encourage young people to cultivate their true, weird, curious, creative, engaging, wonderful selves. As the organization's director and spokesperson, Meredith plays host to a party we all want to attend, with camps, workshops, and service days. She's bringing her talents as a producer to creating Smart Girls video shorts and podcasts.

MINDY KALING

{BORN 1979}

WRITER • PRODUCER • DIRECTOR

This fresh face of comedy first won acclaim for her impersonation of Ben Affleck in an off-Broadway show she wrote. She went on to become the first female writer for *The Office*, a hit mockumentary series in which she was also part of the ensemble cast. Since then, Mindy has created her own acclaimed series— with storylines inspired by her Indian ob-gyn mother—and continued to put pen to paper, writing best-selling books that are simply too funny to put down.

"Sometimes you just have to put on lip gloss and pretend to be psyched."

MINDY KALING
COMEDIAN

SHE LEADS

WILMA MANKILLER

{1945-2010}

INDIGENOUS RIGHTS LEADER • COMMUNITY ORGANIZER •
POLITICIAN

After forced relocation, divorce, and a devastating car crash, the young Wilma followed a calling back to her ancestral home in the Cherokee Nation. There, the optimistic community organizer won out over deep-rooted traditions to eventually be elected as its first female principal chief. The nation's population tripled under Wilma's watch as she empowered her people to tap into their tenacity—shaped by tribal history and heritage—to create "indigenous solutions" to community and personal challenges.

"The most fulfilled people
are those who get up
every morning and stand
for something larger
than themselves."

WILMA MANKILLER
TRIBAL CHIEF

QUEEN LILI'UOKALANI
{1838–1917}

MUSICIAN • PROLIFIC COMPOSER • ROYALTY

This daughter of a Polynesian high chief became the first and only female ruler of Hawaii. She also became her country's last monarch after her attempt to regain power from U.S. business interests led to a military intervention that forced her to give up the throne. The queen who advocated for her people until her dying day continues to be a popular symbol of Hawaiian independence and traditional culture. "Ahola 'Oe," the bittersweet ballad she wrote while under house arrest, remains an island favorite.

"You must remember
never to cease to act
because you fear
you may fail."

QUEEN LILI'UOKALANI
MONARCH

PHUMZILE MLAMBO-NGCUKA
{BORN 1955}

TEACHER • POLITICIAN • EXECUTIVE DIRECTOR OF UN WOMEN

Phumzile, a community development worker who grew up under apartheid, got her start in politics as a cabinet member for Nelson Mandela before becoming South Africa's first female deputy president. Being named the UN's undersecretary general made Phumzile the highest-ranking government official in her home country's history. Today, this global catalyst for gender equity is paving the way for Planet 50/50 by 2030 as the action-oriented head of UN Women.

"My mother always told me that inaction is not an option. And neither is going it alone."

PHUMZILE MLAMBO-NGCUKA
GLOBAL WOMEN'S RIGHTS LEADER

GINNI ROMETTY

{BORN 1957}

COMPUTER SCIENTIST · BUSINESS STRATEGIST · IT INDUSTRY EXEC

Ginni credits her single mom's work ethic for providing inspiration to simply do what needs to be done. She joined IBM as a systems engineer, then three decades later was named as its first female president, chairperson, and CEO. Ginni's time at the head of Big Blue—a global corporation with nearly four hundred thousand employees and $82 billion in annual revenue—has come with complex acquisitions and required tough decisions. Her leadership is ensuring IBM's rich tech and R&D heritage helps harness data, the new natural resource, and advance artificial intelligence to best serve mankind in the digital age. A recurring name on annual Most Admired lists, Ginni is a visible role model who is shaping twenty-first-century business.

"Growth and comfort
never coexist."

GINNI ROMETTY
CHAIRPERSON & CEO

MELLODY HOBSON

{BORN 1969}

FINANCIAL INDUSTRY EXEC • "COLOR BRAVE" CHAMPION • BOARD CHAIR

From a humble Chicago beginning, Mellody worked her way from intern to president at Ariel Investments, the largest minority-owned investment firm. She has shattered stereotypes to become chairperson and member of high-powered boards—from Starbucks to DreamWorks Animation—and a leader when it comes to straight talk about race relations. It's a tough issue, which is exactly why Mellody thinks we need to find the courage to "go there" together, taking action every day in schools and offices, and from local coffee shops to the big screen.

"Hard work plus bravery equals…success. Imagination plus bravery equals…creativity. Love plus bravery equals…happiness."

MELLODY HOBSON
INVESTOR

SHE LOVES

ELIZABETH BARRETT BROWNING
{1806-1861}

This self-taught daughter of English plantation owners was dubbed the "poet laureate" among the Barrett's twelve children. She wrote her first poem at age six and published her first at thirteen. The precocious Christian poet had become a reclusive invalid when the dashing young bard Robert Browning began wooing her in letters. Elizabeth eloped with her talented admirer against her family's wishes. Their romance inspired some of the most soaring love poetry ever written—sonnets that secured Elizabeth's status as the most prominent female author of her day.

"I love thee to the depth and breadth and height my soul can reach."

ELIZABETH BARRETT BROWNING
WRITER

MARIA SHRIVER
{BORN 1955}

NEWS ANCHOR • AUTHOR • "ARCHITECT OF CHANGE"

Whether as a reporter or news correspondent, organizer or executive producer, Maria has focused much of her work on making progress for women in their personal and professional lives. Her award-winning Shriver Reports offer provocative national studies of societal changes that affect women at home and in the workforce. As California's first lady, she launched The Women's Conference, one of the United States' top leadership forums. Today, her organization empowers "architects of change" year-round with grants and awards to recognize everyday change-makers. Among Maria's other close-to-her-heart causes: Special Olympics (founded by her mother, Eunice Kennedy Shriver) and Alzheimer's advocacy (in honor of her father, Peace Corps founding director Sargent Shriver, who died from the disease).

"I'm learning to step back, let go, and watch my daughter soar."

MARIA SHRIVER
JOURNALIST

EMILY DICKINSON

{1830–1886}

Nicknamed the Belle of Amherst, this private intellectual didn't leave her family's estate much as an adult, but she kept up epic correspondence in letters and care packages with her dear ones. Emily's friends and relatives knew she wrote, but they didn't know much or how well. That is, until her sister uncovered a mountain of manuscripts after her death—1,789 untitled poems written in a style and grammar so inventive that early publishers only presented highly edited versions. The rest of us didn't fully catch on to her unconventional genius for several more decades. She is now counted among the defining authors of American literature and the world's best-loved poets.

"My friends are my 'estate.'"

EMILY DICKINSON
POET

MARÍA GREVER

{1885-1951}

LYRICIST • MULTI-INSTRUMENTALIST • MUSIC TEACHER

As Mexico's first professional female composer, María scored many hits with her romantic boleros, catchy habaneras, and tango-infused tunes. Her first published sheet music sold more than three million copies, and her fan base expanded across the Americas when she moved to New York City, where she was tapped to write for the era's top crooners and mentor up-and-comers. The talented pianist's pop repertoire was used for stage shows and film scores, as well as recorded by everyone from Benny Goodman to Aretha Franklin to Gloria Estefan. But it was Dinah Washington's 1959 cover of "What a Difference a Day Makes" that earned María's best-known track a spot in the Grammy Hall of Fame.

"Look, look–because seeing myself in your eyes, I forge such beautiful dreams."

MARÍA GREVER
COMPOSER

MIHRI HATUN
{CIRCA 1460-1506}

JUDGE'S DAUGHTER • SCHOLAR • OTTOMAN AUTHOR

Mihri had a rare thing for an early modern woman—an education. She lived according to the belief that intellect, not gender, determines a person's potential. Her lessons in literature and religion earned her a spot in a prince's inner circle, where she penned bold love poems, championed freethinking and competed with male poets to win rich awards. The height of her career? Becoming the first Muslim woman to present her collected poetry to an admiring sultan.

"At one glance
I loved you with a
thousand hearts."

MIHRI HATUN
POET

SHE OVERCOMES

GABBY GIFFORDS
{BORN 1970}

BUSINESSWOMAN • SURVIVOR • U.S. CONGRESSPERSON

During a meeting with constituents in Gabby's Arizona district, a lone gunman attempted to assassinate this U.S. congressperson. Six people died; thirteen were injured. Gabby was shot in the head. Since that day, she has inspired the nation with her incredible recovery from the traumatic brain injury. Besides taking on rehabilitation with dogged determination, she has continued her commitment to public service, cofounding an organization alongside her astronaut husband to promote common sense gun control measures. While she now struggles to get the words out, those that she shares bear a soulful reminder of how far she has come.

"Be passionate.

Be courageous.

Be your best."

GABBY GIFFORDS
ACTIVIST

HELEN KELLER
{1880-1968}

FIRST DEAF AND BLIND COLLEGE GRAD • PROLIFIC AUTHOR •
SPOKESPERSON FOR THE AMERICAN FEDERATION FOR THE BLIND

A childhood illness left Helen deaf and blind. Nicknamed Little Bronco for her frequent tantrums, she reawakened to the world with the help of her tireless teacher and lifelong companion Anne Sullivan. Helen spent the rest of her extraordinary life using the voice she found to bring light to others as an internationally known author and lecturer. She became a high-profile social justice crusader with causes from socialism to suffrage to children's welfare. At a time when institutionalization was the norm, Helen forever changed attitudes about people with disabilities.

"The world is moved along not only by the mighty shoves of its heroes, but also by the aggregate of the tiny pushes of each honest worker."

HELEN KELLER
HUMANITARIAN

FRIDA KAHLO
{1907–1954}

SURVIVOR • STYLE ICON • SELF-PORTRAIT PAINTER

Frida was no stranger to pain. Her leg was crippled by polio and her body shattered in multiple places by a freak bus crash. She faced heartbreaks and miscarriages. But she never stopped living according to her own avant-garde rules. The painter translated suffering and passion into groundbreaking art inspired by the indigenous culture of her native Mexico. Vibrant, shocking, and heavy with symbolism, Frida's self-portraits earned her acclaim during her lifetime, and then revived her to modern-day cult status. Her bold and quirky style re-entered pop culture in 2004 when a time capsule of her clothing was opened fifty years after her death. One of the world's most ubiquitous female artists, Frida developed iconic imagery that appears in exclusive art exhibitions, across social media, and on a host of everyday goods.

"Feet, what do I need you for when I have wings to fly?"

FRIDA KAHLO
ARTIST

SONIA MANZANO

{BORN 1950}

TV SCRIPTWRITER • FIFTEEN-TIME EMMY WINNER •
MARIA FROM *SESAME STREET*'S "FIX-IT SHOP"

Sonia spent forty-four years as an actor and writer for the world's most popular children's TV program, *Sesame Street*, a show she longed for as a kid. A chaotic childhood made her turn to TV for solace from the violence and alcoholism at home, but she didn't see anyone like her or any place like her Bronx neighborhood on the small screen. After discovering her love of performing arts in high school, Sonia became one of the first Latinas to appear on mainstream media when she was hired to play Maria as her first professional gig. She eventually picked up a pen to write for the program, tapping into the power held by people behind the camera to ensure today's kids see themselves better reflected in society at large.

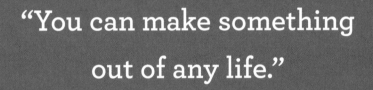

"You can make something
out of any life."

SONIA MANZANO
ACTOR

ADRIANNE HASLET
{BORN 1980}

BOMBING SURVIVOR • HEALTH-CARE ADVOCATE • BIONIC BALLROOM DANCER

This professional dance instructor lost her leg in the Boston Marathon bombing. Adrianne's life may have been irreparably changed in a second's time, but her recovery process created a community of survivors which gave others the opportunity to deal with tragedy. Determined to thrive, she made good on her vow to return to the dance floor in less than a year, debuting new prosthetic technology from the MIT Media Lab's Biomechatronics Group. Today, she can add long-distance runner and mountaineer to her list of accomplishments. Besides scaling one of Ecuador's highest peaks, Adrianne returned to the Boston Marathon just three years after her life took a turn, courageously crossing the finish line of the grueling twenty-six-mile course.

"I refuse to be called a victim.
I am not defined
by what happened in my life.
I am a survivor, defined
by how I live my life."

ADRIANNE HASLET
DANCER

SHE PIONEERS

JULIETTE GORDON LOW
{1860-1927}

**PHILANTHROPIST • DISABILITY ADVOCATE (SHE WAS PARTIALLY DEAF) •
THE ORIGINAL GIRL SCOUT**

Nicknamed Daisy during her Savannah childhood, this game changer for girls founded the Girl Scouts of USA in 1912, serving as its leader and primary funder for fifteen years. Inspired by the UK's Boy Scout movement while in London, Juliette returned home to start a national program of her own designed to groom young women for leadership roles. More than a century and fifty million scouts in 145 countries later, Juliette's troops are still fostering independent, courageous girls who're stepping up to be tomorrow's top execs in all fields. While badges for achievement reflect values that go back to the early days, today's Scouts are up to date: camping and crafts are offered alongside coding and designing online cookie storefronts.

"The work of today is the history of tomorrow, and we are its makers."

JULIETTE GORDON LOW
GIRL SCOUTS FOUNDER

LAURA INGALLS WILDER

{1867-1957}

PIONEER GIRL • DAIRY FARMER • CHILDREN'S BOOK AUTHOR

Laura lived in the woods, on the prairie, and at a farm of her very own. During the Great Depression, sixty-two-year-old Laura sat down at her two-hundred-acre Rocky Ridge Farm to write her memoirs. Sixty million copies later, the Little House series that recounts Laura's youth on the American frontier continues to be a staple of children's literature. With everyday survival tales that take us from log cabins to dugouts, Laura's books still speak to a simpler way of life built on hard work, self-sufficiency, and pulling together. Her loving accounts of her close-knit and sensible Ingalls family have touched millions worldwide.

"It is the simple things of life that make living worthwhile, the sweet fundamental things such as love and duty, work and rest, and living close to nature."

LAURA INGALLS WILDER
WRITER

BILLIE JEAN KING
{BORN 1943}

TWELVE-TIME GRAND-SLAM SINGLES WINNER • PAY EQUITY CHAMPION • NAMESAKE OF THE USTA CENTER, HOME TO THE U.S. OPEN

Tennis champ Billie Jean was not yet thirty when she accepted a challenge from a male pro, taking her convictions to the court in the 1973 spectacle called the Battle of the Sexes. She knew what was at stake. Just one year after the historic Title IX legislation passed, the match was timely and visible evidence that female athletes could compete . . . and win! The very same year, this trailblazer founded the Women's Tennis Association to organize other female pros. Since then, Billie Jean has continued to serve up Ws for gender equality. From cofounding the Women's Sports Federation to launching a leadership initiative for the promotion of diversity and inclusion in the workplace, she is intent on ensuring tennis does not remain the only pro sport (or profession) with pay parity.

"Pressure is a privilege."

BILLIE JEAN KING
TENNIS PLAYER

HILLARY RODHAM CLINTON
{BORN 1947}

FIRST LADY · SENATOR · SECRETARY OF STATE

This former lawyer has spent thirty-plus years in public service. After starting her career with the Children's Defense Fund, Hillary taught law in Arkansas before becoming the state's first lady for twelve years. As a two-term first lady of the United States, she boldly championed her own political initiatives— from gender equity to gun control to health care reform. Since then, she has served as a U.S. senator from New York and the 67th secretary of state, and ran for the presidency twice. Hillary's second primary battle saw her make history— as the first female presidential nominee from a major party.

"When women succeed,
the world succeeds.
When women and girls thrive,
entire societies thrive.
Just as women's rights
are human rights, women's
progress is human progress."

HILLARY RODHAM CLINTON
POLITICIAN

ANN DUNWOODY

{BORN 1953}

LOGISTICIAN · FIRST FEMALE FOUR-STAR ARMY GENERAL · LEADERSHIP EXPERT

This army brat joined up to "jump out of airplanes for two years" and ended up serving for thirty-seven. By the time Ann retired, she had four stars across her lapel—the ultimate earned honor for the commanding general of the U.S. Army Materiel Command. Her outfit equips soldiers with everything when and where they need it. That includes a $60 billion supply chain operation with sixty-nine thousand employees in 145 countries. Today, she's sharing leadership lessons learned from her nearly four-decade-long military career. And proudly seeing more girls who now know there's a path.

"A hero is an everyday, ordinary person who has done something extraordinary. Honor them, praise them, and hope you will stand for what you believe in during a time of need."

ANN DUNWOODY
GENERAL

MISTY COPELAND

{BORN 1982}

LATE-BLOOMING DANCER • AWARD-WINNING AUTHOR • VIRAL SENSATION

If not for being coaxed to join a ballet class at a local Boys & Girls Club, thirteen-year-old Misty might never have uncovered her passion and talent for classical dance. An atypical ballerina body didn't keep her from becoming a toe-shoe–wearing triumph whose performances have wowed in everything from *Firebird* to *Swan Lake*. As the first African-American principal dancer at the American Ballet Theatre, she has become a pop-culture icon. Her ongoing story is chronicled through stunning videos, visuals, and texts that nudge us to pursue our own passions, even if they take us down unexpected paths.

"You can start late,
look different, be uncertain,
and still succeed."

MISTY COPELAND
BALLERINA

SHE PRESERVES

RACHEL CARSON

{1907-1964}

SCIENCE EDITOR • BIOLOGIST • ECO-REVOLUTIONARY

Rachel's gift for writing surfaced when she began inking radio scripts as a junior marine biologist at the U.S. Bureau of Fisheries. Her lyrical style and sentimental narratives carried through three popular books about the wonders of the sea, including the award-winning best seller, *The Sea Around Us*. Her 1962 book, *Silent Spring*, documented the effects of the agriculture industry on songbird populations. Rachel researched and wrote the influential critique that kick-started the environmental movement while battling breast cancer and caring for a young child. Though her work stirred up controversy, the quiet leader showed courage in the aftermath. Rachel's efforts led to a ban on the harmful pesticide DDT and the creation of the Environmental Protection Agency.

"One way to open your eyes
is to ask yourself,
'What if I had never
seen this before?
What if I knew I would
never see it again?'"

RACHEL CARSON
ENVIRONMENTALIST

MARJORY STONEMAN DOUGLAS

{1890-1998}

AUTHOR • ENVIRONMENTALIST • GRAND DAME OF THE EVERGLADES

Marjory turned a chance editorial assignment on the Miami River into a passion-driven career protecting the Sunshine State's one-of-a-kind River of Grass. Over five decades, she transformed the Everglades from little-known swamp to treasured national park and site of one of the world's largest restoration projects. The attention she brought to this unique ecosystem kept it from being drained and converted into yet another housing or corporate development. Feisty to the end, Marjory passed away at age 108. The tiny Coconut Grove cottage where she penned her action-inspiring essays is now a designated national landmark.

"I believe that life should be lived so vividly and so intensely that thoughts of another life, or of a longer life, are not necessary."

MARJORY STONEMAN DOUGLAS
WRITER

SONIA SOTOMAYOR

{BORN 1954}

"A CHILD WITH DREAMS" • LAWYER • JUDGE

Sonia had a lot to overcome to get where she is today as the first Latina appointed to preserve the intent of the Constitution at the U.S. Supreme Court. The associate justice's early challenges—poverty, childhood diabetes, being raised by a single mom, discrimination—inspired her passion for public service. From her days as a student civil rights activist to her first gig as a New York assistant district attorney to her tenure as the third woman to serve on the nation's top bench, Sonia has maintained a calm determination to ensure the law serves everyone.

"Don't mistake politeness
for lack of strength."

SONIA SOTOMAYOR
SUPREME COURT JUSTICE

GRACE YOUNG

{BORN 1956}

TEST KITCHEN DIRECTOR • JAMES BEARD AWARD WINNER • POET LAUREATE OF THE WOK

Despite being raised in a family of Cantonese home cooks, Grace grew up idolizing Julia Child and studying French cuisine. She started her culinary career running the test kitchen for Time-Life cookbooks. It wasn't until this New Yorker returned to her Bay Area culinary heritage that she found her true calling as a chef—to be a wok evangelist. Today, she has three award-winning cookbooks that celebrate and preserve the wisdom of the Chinese kitchen while teaching foodies everywhere how to wok their way to the perfect stir-fry. Her personal observation: as her own family ages, the aromas and flavors from favorite recipes passed down for generations stir memories and prompt conversations that might otherwise be lost.

"Preserve your culinary legacy. Someday those recipes could be the one link we have to reach our loved ones."

GRACE YOUNG
CHEF

SARAH LEWIS

{BORN 1979}

AUTHOR • MUSEUM CURATOR • ART HISTORY PROFESSOR

Sarah began her career in art when she entered a national competition put on by the NAACP. The teen's still life earned top honors and a face-to-face with Rosa Parks at the awards ceremony. Since then, Sarah has lived out her love of art through museum curation and university research. With a book that explores how failure is central to the creative process, this Harvard professor's work has reached well beyond her field, inspiring inventors and entrepreneurs to embrace the slow but fulfilling pursuit of mastery.

"Success is a moment,
but what we're always celebrating
is creativity and mastery."

SARAH LEWIS
HISTORIAN

SHE TEACHES

MARY MCLEOD BETHUNE

{1875–1955}

CIVIL RIGHTS LEADER • TEACHER • COLLEGE PRESIDENT

Called the First Lady of Struggle, Mary was an all-out champion of the rights of African-American women, whom she lovingly referred to as her "daughters." The child of former slaves turned working poor, she was the only one of seventeen siblings to attend school. Driven by the conviction that education was essential to racial equality, Mary spent ten years as a teacher, opening her first school in Florida with a capital investment of just $1.50. That school ultimately became a college that still bears her name. This educator's impact reached well beyond her own campus. She founded a civil rights organization, advised four U.S. presidents, and championed social causes alongside her dear friend Eleanor Roosevelt.

"Any idea that keeps anybody out is too small."

MARY MCLEOD BETHUNE
UNIVERSITY FOUNDER

PEMA CHÖDRÖN
{BORN 1936}

EDUCATOR · AUTHOR · TIBETAN BUDDHIST SPIRITUAL LEADER

Pema had a life as an English teacher, married with two small children, when a series of personal heartbreaks led her to seek spiritual answers to suffering. The first American to be ordained a Buddhist nun in the Vajrayana tradition, Pema also became the inaugural director of North America's first Tibetan monastery for Westerners. Today, she teaches about how to approach our difficult "attachments" from Nova Scotia's Gampo Abbey. With a given name that means "lamp of truth," Pema is a guiding light in the realm of contemporary spirituality.

"Nothing ever goes away
until it has taught us
what we need to know."

PEMA CHÖDRÖN
NUN

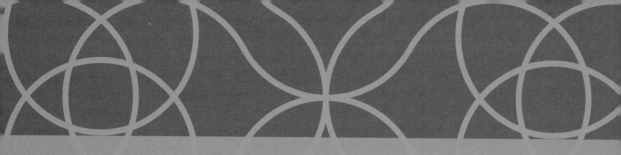

JO BOALER
{BORN 1964}

MATH TEACHER · EDUCATION PROFESSOR · NONPROFIT FOUNDER

British-born Jo is revolutionizing the math classroom by changing students' attitudes toward the reputedly tough subject. Her research shows that the most important arithmetic lesson to boost success is being trained to embrace mistakes as a key part of learning. Through a nonprofit called YouCubed that's dedicated to putting the latest techniques and resources into educators' hands, this Stanford professor is helping all kids (even those who typically opt out of math and science class) become genuine numbers people.

"Mistakes grow your brain."

JO BOALER
MATHEMATICIAN

ANGELA DUCKWORTH
{BORN 1970}

TEACHER · MACARTHUR GENIUS · PSYCHOLOGIST OF SUCCESS

Angela had transitioned from the world of management consulting to teaching seventh-grade math in poor urban neighborhoods when she wondered: Why don't intelligent, gifted students do as well as hardworking students? The question took her out of the classroom and into the research lab to figure out the science behind success in school. Angela's findings confirmed her hunch: "Character is at least as important as intellect." If self-discipline trumps IQ and talent as a predictor of achievement, that's good news for educators because "grit" is a trait that can be taught. Now this Penn professor is working with both the Gates and MacArthur Foundations to find the best way to groom gritty kids so they're destined for success.

"Grit is sticking with your future, day in, day out, not just for the week, not just for the month, but for years, and working really hard to make that future a reality. Grit is living life like it's a marathon, not a sprint."

ANGELA DUCKWORTH
RESEARCH PSYCHOLOGIST

RESHMA SAUJANI
{BORN 1975}

LAWYER · NONPROFIT FOUNDER · POLITICIAN

Reshma founded Girls Who Code to close the gender gap in technology. Today, the STEM education program engages forty thousand girls through 1,500 clubs and attracts big-name companies eager to create a future shaped by diverse tech talent. Reshma is not a coder herself, but she's always been interested in advancing women in leadership. The Wall Street lawyer who became the first Indian-American woman to run for U.S. Congress is a model for embracing risk and failure. She's championing a brave new world to counteract a culture where girls are held back by expecting themselves to be "perfect."

"Code breaks and then it falls apart, and it often takes many, many tries until that magical moment when what you're trying to build comes to life. It requires perseverance. It requires imperfection."

RESHMA SAUJANI
STEM EDUCATOR

SHE WRITES

MARY SHELLEY
{1797-1851}

DAYDREAMER · SCANDALOUS ROMANTIC ·
SCI-FI AND HORROR GENRE PIONEER

The daughter of two famous radical political philosophers and the wife of a poet, Mary didn't write much herself, until gloomy weather kept Mary and friends cooped up inside a Swiss lake house during the Year Without a Summer. The frustrated vacationers passed the time with a ghost story contest that sparked the teen's imagination, so she dreamed up *Frankenstein*. The story brought Mary a reputation in the world of literature to match that of her parents and husband. The novel's message—beware, lest you create a monster— couldn't be more relevant in today's science-fiction reality.

"Invention, it must be humbly admitted, does not consist in creating out of void, but out of chaos."

MARY SHELLEY
AUTHOR

LORRAINE HANSBERRY

{1930–1965}

JOURNALIST • CIVIL RIGHTS WORKER • PAINTER

Lorraine's very first play made it to Broadway when she was only twenty-eight. It was a debut that completely transformed American theater by opening doors, stages, and screens to African-American playwrights, actors, and directors. Based on her real-life experiences growing up in segregated Chicago, Lorraine's acclaimed drama, *A Raisin in the Sun*, is still reaching new audiences through award-winning revivals. Sadly, this celebrated playwright's promising career was cut short by cancer.

"You have something glorious to draw on begging for attention. Don't pass it up. Use it."

LORRAINE HANSBERRY
PLAYWRIGHT

ARIANNA HUFFINGTON

{BORN 1950}

BLOGGER • TRAILBLAZING DIGITAL PUBLISHER • WELLNESS CHAMPION

Arianna is best known for pioneering digital-only journalism through her Huffington Post, an upstart blog that's become one of the United States' go-to news sites. The ubiquitous Arianna has been an author, a radio show host, a political commentator, a politician, and a self-help guru over the course of her forty-year career. Today, this entrepreneurial Greek expat is on a mission to redefine success by adding a crucial "third metric"—well-being. Her own startling health crisis turned her into a sleep crusader, reminding us to put away the electronics and tuck into bed to give our minds much-needed regenerative rest. She has stepped away from her publishing empire to focus full time on fostering healthy environments where individuals can thrive.

"The enemy of wonder
is multitasking."

ARIANNA HUFFINGTON
JOURNALIST

J.K. ROWLING

{BORN 1965}

UNEMPLOYED SECRETARY • BEST-SELLING NOVELIST • WIZARD WITH WORDS

Joanne Rowling was a single mother struggling to provide for her daughter when she had a vision of the boy wizard who would become one of most adored characters of all time. It took seven years for a small press to take a chance on her *Harry Potter* series, but its instant success was the start of an entertainment empire complete with best-selling novels, blockbuster films, theme parks, and gear. Under her pen name, J.K. Rowling, she has inspired generations to love reading (and rereading!) while they wait for the next tale to be spun. Her many good works have transformed the world by giving back to fans, empowering single parents, supporting medical research, and caring for underprivileged orphans like Harry.

"We do not need magic to transform our world. We carry all the power we need inside ourselves already: we have the power to imagine better."

J.K. ROWLING
AUTHOR

ISABEL ALLENDE
{BORN 1942}

FEMINIST JOURNALIST • MEMOIRIST • FOUNDATION FOUNDER

Isabel was in exile from her native Chile as a political refugee when news that her hundred-year-old grandfather was dying inspired her to write her first best-selling novel, *The House of the Spirits*. The multigenerational epic launched her career as one of the most widely read Spanish-language authors, known for her "tales of passion." When she lost her only daughter to illness, Isabel coped by carrying on Paula's personal philosophy: "You only have what you give." She created a foundation to empower women and girls around the world, launching it with the proceeds from her soul-baring memoir penned over the course of the year Paula died.

"Stuff is irrelevant. Sooner or later we have to throw overboard our possessions, vanities, and ambitions; only the good we have done matters."

ISABEL ALLENDE
NOVELIST

PERMISSIONS

{ GOOD MANNERS MATTER }

"The best way
to honor a blessing is
to be a blessing."

MPUMI NOBIVA
GRAD STUDENT

We respect the rights of the people and organizations behind original thinking. It's why we go to great lengths to fact-check and give credit where credit is due.

Quotes are often considered fair use, and many of the selections in the book are in the public domain. We took an added step to proactively seek permission for contemporary quotations. And we diligently worked to ensure this collection reflected diversity—of ideas, beliefs, era, culture, geography, career paths, partnering choices, and so on.

We were delighted that we heard directly from many women and girls featured in our book! We're also truly grateful for the support of the many foundation execs, team members, publicists, agents, assistants, advisors, legal counsels, and permissions departments at the organizations who steered us in the right direction. You helped us dot the i's and cross the t's to ensure approvals are properly in place.

A sincere thanks to the people who said "yes":

SHE BELIEVES
Dorothy Day via The Catholic Worker • Marianne Williamson via MarianneWilliamson.com • Sharon Salzberg via Penguin Publishing Group

SHE BUILDS
Dame Zaha Hadid via Zaha Hadid Architects • Sheila Johnson via Salamander Hotels and Resorts • Linda Alvarado and Alvarado Construction and the Colorado Rockies • Debbie Sterling via the public relations agency of GoldieBlox

SHE CHAMPIONS
Rosa Parks via Penguin Publishing Group • Gloria Steinem via GloriaSteinem.com • Shirin Ebadi via the Global Fund for Women • Ertharin Cousin via the World Food Programme

SHE COACHES
Emily Post via Lizzie Post, president of the Emily Post Institute • Julia Child via The Julia Child Foundation for Gastronomy and the Culinary Arts, coauthor Alex Prud'homme and Alfred A. Knopf / Penguin Random House • Dr. Joyce Brothers via Parade magazine • Martha Karolyi • Marie Kondo via konmari.com

SHE COMPETES
Mia Hamm via the Mia Hamm Foundation • Dame Ellen MacArthur via the Ellen MacArthur Foundation • Serena Williams via her publicist and agent • Jamie Anderson • Ashima Shiraishi via her agent

SHE DESIGNS
Coco Chanel via Little, Brown • Dorothy Draper via Carleton Varney, president of Dorothy Draper & Company • Juliane Blasi and the BMW Group • Monique Péan

SHE DISCOVERS
Zora Neale Hurston via Harper Collins • Dr. Sylvia Earle via Mission Blue • Dr. Leslie Gordon via the Progeria Research Foundation • Dr. Sarah Parcak

SHE ENTERTAINS
Mae West via Prentice-Hall • Ella Fitzgerald via CMG Worldwide • Geena Davis via the Geena Davis Institute on Gender in Media • Shonda Rhimes via her legal counsel

SHE EXPLORES
Dr. Mae Jemison via the Dorothy Jemison Foundation for Excellence • Alison Levine • Léa Brassy

SHE GIVES
Anne Frank via Anne Frank Fonds • Audrey Hepburn via Sean Hepburn Ferrer, author of Audrey Hepburn, An Elegant Spirit • Melinda Gates via the Bill and Melinda Gates Foundation • Oprah Winfrey via OWN

SHE HEALS
Dr. Margaret Chan via the World Heath Organization • Dame Claire Bertschinger • Dr. Brené Brown via the Brené Brown Research and Education Group

SHE INSPIRES
Eleanor Roosevelt via the Roosevelt Institute • Amelia Earhart via CMG Worldwide • Maya Angelou via MayaAngelou.com • Malala Yousafzai via the Malala Fund

SHE INVENTS
Dr. Temple Grandin via Colorado State University • Robin Chase • Danae Ringelmann via Indiegogo

SHE LAUGHS
Lucille Ball via CBS Radio • Rosario Castellanos via University of Texas Press • Amy Poehler via her agents and Amy Poehler's Smart Girls • Meredith Walker via Amy Poehler's Smart Girls • Mindy Kaling via Three Rivers Press / Random House

SHE LEADS

Wilma Mankiller via the Wilma Mankiller Foundation • Phumzile Mlambo-Ngcuka via UN Women • Ginni Rometty via IBM Corp. • Mellody Hobson via Ariel Investments

SHE LOVES

Maria Shriver via Shriver Media

SHE OVERCOMES

Frida Kahlo via Abrams • Sonia Manzano • Gabby Giffords via Americans for Responsible Solutions • Adrianne Haslet via her public relations agency

SHE PIONEERS

Billie Jean King via her publicist • Retired General Ann Dunwoody • Misty Copeland via her publicist

SHE PRESERVES

Marjory Stoneman Douglas via Pineapple Press, Inc. • Rachel Carson via Harper Collins • Justice Sonia Sotomayor via the Public Information Office, Supreme Court of the United States • Grace Young • Dr. Sarah Lewis

SHE TEACHES

Pema Chödrön via Shambhala Publications • Dr. Jo Boaler • Dr. Angela Duckworth via AngelaDuckworth.com • Reshma Saujani via Girls Who Code

SHE WRITES

Lorraine Hansberry via her agent • Arianna Huffington via The Huffington Post Media Group • J.K. Rowling via her agent • Isabel Allende via IsabelAllende.com

PERMISSIONS

Mpumi Nobiva

BIBLIOGRAPHY

Adora Svitak via AdoraSvitak.com

BIBLIOGRAPHY

{ SOURCE IT! }

BELIEVES

Day, Dorothy. "Aims and Purposes." The Catholic Worker, February 1940.

Hildegard of Bingen. Causes and Cures. ca. 1151. Hildegard of Bingen: A Spiritual Reader. Ed. Carmen Acevedo Butcher. Paraclete Press, 2007.

Shaker Testimonies of the Life, Character, Revelations and Doctrines of Mother Ann Lee, and the Elders with Her. The Shakers, 1816.

Williamson, Marianne. A Return to Love. HarperCollins, 1992.

Salzberg, Sharon. Faith: Trusting in Your Own Deepest Experience. Penguin, 2002.

BUILDS

Walker, Madam CJ. "Speech at Fifteenth Annual Convention of the National Negro Business League." 1914. Hair Story. Ayana Byrd and Lori Tharps. St. Martin Griffins, 2001.

Hattenstone, Simon. "Master Builder." The Guardian: Architecture, February 3, 2003. www.theguardian.com/artanddesign/2003/feb/03/architecture.artsfeatures.

Fales-Hill, Susan. "Sheila's Third Act." Essence 44.9, January 2014.

"Linda Alvarado." Hispanic Scholarship Fund. 2016. http://hsf.net/en/media/hsf-stories/linda-alvarado.

O'Connor, Clare. "GoldieBlox's Debbie Sterling Engineers STEM Breakthrough." Forbes, October 2014. www.forbes.com/video/3818040528001.

CHAMPIONS

Watson, Emma. "The Graduate." Interview with Jenny Dickinson. Elle, August 2009

Stanton, Elizabeth Cady. "To the Women's Convention." May 25, 1851. The Female Experience. Ed. Gerda Lerner. Oxford University Press, 1977.

Parks, Rosa. Rosa Parks: My Story. With Jim Haskins. Puffin Books, 1998.

Steinem, Gloria. "Moving Beyond Words." Ford Hall Forum, May 12, 1994. FORA.tv. http://library.fora.TV/1994/05/12/Gloria_Steinem_Moving_Beyond_Words.

Samini, Ali, and Ashraf Zahedia. "Pioneer in Peace: An Interview with Nobel Peace Prize Winner Shirin Ebadi." Global Fund for Women's Muslima: Muslim Women's Art & Voices. http://muslima.globalfundforwomen.org/content/pioneer-peace. Accessed September 1, 2016.

Cousin, Ertharin. "Closing Remarks by Executive Director Ms. Ertharin Cousin on the Occasion of the Second Regular Session of the WFP Executive Board." November 8, 2013. World Food Programme. www.wfp.org/eds-centre/speeches/closing-remarks-executive-director-ms-ertharin-cousin-occasion-second-regular-se.

COACHES

Post, Emily. Etiquette. Funk & Wagnalls, 1922.

Child, Julia, and Alex Prud'Homme. My Life in France. Anchor, 2007.

Brothers, Joyce. "You Can Lead a More Joyful Life." Parade, October 15, 2000.

"Interview: Marta Karolyi." International Gymnast, September 2006.

Kondo, Marie. The Life-Changing Magic of Tidying Up. Ten Speed Press, 2014.

COMPETES

Downing, Erin. For Soccer-Crazy Girls Only. Feiwel and Friends, 2014, 20.

McArthur, Ellen. "The Surprising Thing I Learned Sailing Solo Around the World." TED2015, March 2015. www.ted.com/talks/

dame_ellen_macarthur_the_surprising_thing_i_learned_sailing_solo_around_the_world?language=en.

Coulton, Antoinette. "Here's How to Take a Tennis Masterclass with Serena Williams." People, May 12, 2015. http://people.com/celebrity/heres-how-to-take-a-tennis-masterclass-with-serena-williams.

"Jamie Anderson in Only a Smile." ESPN Magazine: The Body Issue, June 2014.

Michelson, Megan. "A Conversation with Two of the Most Powerful Teens in Climbing." Outside, March 15, 2016. www.outsideonline.com/2061271/conversation-two-most-powerful-teens-climbing.

DESIGNS

Haedrich, Marcel. Coco Chanel: Her Life, Her Secrets. Little, Brown and Company, 1972.

Draper, Dorothy. Decorating Is Fun! The Literary Guild of America, 1939.

O'Keeffe, Georgia. Exhibition Catalog, Museum of Modern Art, 1943.

Papst, Natascha. "Female Design." Ladies Drive, September 2007.

Mallard, Anne-Sophie. "Monique Péan: A Jewelry Designer with a Conscience." Vogue Paris, April 20, 2016. http://en.vogue.fr/jewelry/profile/diaporama/monique-pean-a-jewelry-designer-with-aconscience/31100#monique-pean-x-trees-for-the-future.

DISCOVERS

Mitchell, Maria. Maria Mitchell: Life, Letters, and Journals. Ed. Phebe Mitchell Kendall. Lee and Shepard, 1896.

Hurston, Zora Neale. Their Eyes Were Watching God. J.B. Lippincott & Co., 1937.

McCord, Meagan. "Gills Club Interviews Dr. Sylvia Earle." Mission Blue: Sylvia Earle Alliance, July 30, 2015. www.mission-blue.org/2015/07/gills-club-interviews-dr-sylvia-earle.

Gordon, Leslie. "The Difference That Makes a Difference." TEDx Charlottesville, 2013. TEDx Talks. www.youtube.com/watch?v=MbJqXHtZaOM.

"Sarah Parcak: Space Archeologist Wizard Genius." The Late Show with Stephen Colbert. CBS, January 8, 2016.

ENTERTAINS

West, Mae. Goodness Had Nothing to Do with It. Prentice-Hall, 1959.

Kellerman, Annette. How to Swim. George H. Doran Company, 1918.

The Official Site of the First Lady of Song. www.ellafitzgerald.com/about/quote.html. Accessed September 1, 2016.

Davis, Geena. "Geena Davis' Two Easy Steps to Make Hollywood Less Sexist." The Hollywood Reporter, December 11, 2013. www.hollywoodreporter.com/news/geena-davis-two-easy-steps-664573.

Rhimes, Shonda. "My Year of Saying Yes to Everything." TED2016, February 2016. www.ted.com/talks/shonda_rhimes_my_year_of_saying_yes_to_everything?language=en.

EXPLORES

Bly, Nellie. Around the World in Seventy-Two Days. The Pictorial Weeklies Company, 1890.

Iversen, Kristen. Molly Brown: Unraveling the Myth. Johnson Books, 1999, 36.

Longenecker, Donna. "Space Exploration Worth Risk, Jemison Says." UB Reporter, March 6, 2003. www.buffalo.edu/ubreporter/archive/vol34/vol34n16/articles/Jemison.html.

Levine, Alison. "Keynote." Power Transmission Distributors Association Industry Summit, 2011.

Ryan, Matthew. "Interview: Lea Brassy—Simple Voyage." SurfCareers, September 22, 2014. http://surfcareers.com/blog/lea-brassy-simple-voyage.

GIVES

Winfrey, Oprah. "Presidential Medal of Freedom Recipient - Oprah Winfrey." The White House, November 22, 2013. https://www.youtube.com/watch?v=7VH4Hp8VJzU.

Smith, Sophia. "Sophia Smith's Journal, 1861–1870: Selected Entries Relating to the Disposition of Her Property." Smith College Archives, April 1, 1997. http://clio.fivecolleges.edu/smith/sophia/who/journal/j_indx.htm.

Frank, Anne. "Give!" March 26 1944. Tales from the Secret Annex. Trans Susan Massotty. Bantam, 2003.

Hepburn Ferrer, Sean. Audrey Hepburn, An Elegant Spirit. Simon & Schuster, 1999, 180.

Gates, Melinda, and Kathy Calvin. "Bring Every Good Thing to Our Children." The Huffington Post, March 31, 2014. www.huffingtonpost.com/melinda-gates/bring-every-good-thing-to_b_5054769.html.

HEALS

Brown, Brené. The Gifts of Imperfection. Hazelton, 2010.

Nightingale, Florence. Notes on Nursing. D. Appleton & Co., 1860.

Blackwell, Elizabeth. Pioneer Work in Opening the Medical Profession to Women. Longmans, Green, and Company, 1895.

Ladd, Anna Coleman. "Being a Sculptor." ca. 1930. Archives of American Art. www.aaa.si.edu/collections/container/viewer/Lecture-about-Being-a-Sculptor-230284.

Chan, Margaret. "Time to Get Back on Track to Meet the Millennium Goals: Address to the Sixty-third World Health Assembly." Geneva, Switzerland, May 17, 2010. www.who.int/dg/speeches/2010/WHA_address_20100517/en.

Bertschinger, Claire, and Fanny Blake. Moving Mountains. Doubleday, 2005.

INSPIRES

Obama, Michelle. "Remarks by the Frist Lady at the National Mentoring Summit." The White House, January 25, 2011.

Humez, Jean. Harriet Tubman: The Life and Stories. University of Wisconsin Press, 2003.

Roosevelt, Eleanor. You Learn by Living. Harper & Brothers, 1960.

The Official Website of Amelia Earhart. www.ameliaearhart.com/about/quotes.html.

Accessed September 1, 2016.

Angelou, Maya. I Know Why the Caged Bird Sings. Random House, 1969.

Yousafzai, Malala. "Address on Malala Day." The United Nations Youth Assembly, New York, July 12, 2013. www.youtube.com/watch?v=3rNhZu3ttIU.

INVENTS

Robin Chase Official Website. www.robinchase.org. Accessed January 15, 2014.

Pilon, Mary. "A Woman Invents." In The Monopolists. Bloomsbury, 2015.

Hopper, Grace. "Lecture by Rear Admiral Grace Hopper as the Head of Training and Technology Directorate at Naval Data Automation Command." Florida, 1987. www.youtube.com/watch?v=9Ra2kt1Mpg8.

Grandin, Temple. "The World Needs All Kinds of Minds." TED2010, February 2010. www.ted.com/talks/temple_grandin_the_world_needs_all_kinds_of_minds?language=en.

Spence, Ewan. "Resistance, Rejection, and Ridicule. Start-up Expectations from Indiegogo's Danae Ringelmann." Forbes, December 2, 2014. www.forbes.com/sites/ewanspence/2014/12/02/interview-indiegogo-crowdfunding-danae-ringelmann/2/#3361b381207f.

LAUGHS

"Behind the Laughter of Jackie (Moms) Mabley." Ebony, August 1962, 89.

Ball, Lucille. "Let's Talk to Lucy." Interview with Doris Day. WBBM, March 22, 1965.

Castellanos, Rosario. "If Not Poetry, Then What?" A Rosario Castellanos Reader. Trans. and ed. Maureen Ahern. University of Texas Press, 1988.

Poehler, Amy. Yes Please. Dey Street, 2014.

Buelvas, Maritza. "Breakfast with Smart Girl and Boss Babe Meredith Walker." In The Longevity Book, by Cameron Diaz. Harper, 2016. www.ourbodybook.com/breakfast-with-smart-girl-meredith-walker.

Kaling, Mindy. Is Everyone Hanging Out without Me? (And Other Concerns). Crown Archetype, 2011.

LEADS

Mankiller, Wilma. Commencement Address. Northeastern State University, May 16, 2009. www.nsuok.edu/News/Story/1082/Default.aspx.

Marsella, Anthony, Jeanette Johnson, Patricia Watson, and Jan Gryczynski. Ethnocultural Perspectives on Disaster and Trauma. Springer, 2008, 274.

Mlambo-Ngcuka, Phumzile. "My Mother Always Told Me Inaction Is Not an Option." The Huffington Post, March 19, 2014. www.huffingtonpost.com/phumzile-mlambongcuka/my-mother-always-told-me-_b_4988671.html.

"Ginny Rometty, President and CEO, IBM." The Economic Club of Washington, D.C., December 3, 2014. www.youtube.com/watch?v=B9brTt_eLPo&t=636.

Hobson, Mellody. "Set Your Sights High." Commencement Address. University of Southern California, May 15, 2015. http://time.com/3889937/mellody-hobson-graduation-speech-usc.

LOVES

Browning, Elizabeth Barrett. "Sonnet XLIII." Sonnets from the Portuguese. 1850. G.P. Putnam's Sons, 1902, 96.

Hatun, Mihri. "At One Glance." Nightingales and Pleasure Gardens: Turkish Love Poems. Trans. and ed. Talât Sait Halman. Syracuse University Press, 2005, 35.

Dickinson, Emily. "Letter to Samuel Bowles." August 1858. Amherst College Archives. www.amherst.edu/library/archives/holdings/edickinson/new_daguerreotype/pattersonriddle.

Grever, María. "Así." Trans. Alicia Williamson. In "Lyríca greveriana." Ed. Ariel Ruiz Mandragón. La insignia, December 15, 2001. www.lainsignia.org/2001/diciembre/cul_028.htm.

"Katherine Schwarzenegger Gets a Surprise Message from Her Mother." The Queen Latifah Show, May 1, 2014. www.youtube.com/watch?v=8uAjjALYLjo.

OVERCOMES

Giffords, Gabby, and Mark Kelly. "Be passionate. Be courageous. Be your best." TED2014, March 2014. www.ted.com/talks/gabby_giffords_and_mark_kelly_be_passionate_be_courageous_be_your_best.

Keller, Helen. Optimism: An Essay. The Merrymount Press, 1903, 21.

Herrera, Hayden. Frida: A Biography of Frida Kahlo. Perennial, 1983, 415.

"2015 ALA Annual Conference—Sonia Manzano on 'Becoming Maria.'" June 30, 2015. www.youtube.com/watch?v=4Mqzd2iIFVA.

Haslet, Adrianne. www.adriannehaslet.com. Accessed September 1, 2016.

PIONEERS

Low, Juliette, and W. J. Hoxie. How Girls Can Help Their Country. The Knickerbocker Press, 1913, 104.

Wilder, Laura Ingalls. "A Bouquet of Wildflowers." The Missouri Ruralist, July 20, 1917.

King, Billie Jean. Pressure Is a Privilege. LifeTime Media, 2008.

Dunwoody, Ann. "Lessons from a Higher Standard: Leadership Strategies from America's First Four-Star General." General Ann Dunwoody, www.pbgsmarttools.com/sites/ahigherstandard/lessons.html. Accessed September 1, 2016.

Copeland, Misty. Life in Motion: An Unlikely Ballerina. Touchstone, 2014, 262.

Clinton, Hillary. "Remarks on the U.N. Commemoration of International Women's Day." The United Nations, March 7, 2014.

PRESERVES

Carson, Rachel. The Sense of Wonder. Harper & Row, 1965.

Douglas, Marjorie Stoneman. Voice of the River. Pineapple Press, 1987, 258.

Totenberg, Nina. "A Justice Deliberates: Sotomayor on Love, Health And Family." NPR Morning Edition, January 12, 2013. www.npr.org/2013/01/14/167699633/a-justice-deliberates-sotomayor-on-love-health-

and-family.

Young, Grace. "Year of the Ram." February 12, 2015. www.graceyoung.com/2015/02/year-of-the-ram.

Lewis, Sarah. "Embrace the Near Win." TED2014, March 2014. www.ted.com/talks/sarah_lewis_embrace_the_near_win?language=en.

TEACHES

Bethune, Mary McLeod. "Address to a World Assembly for Moral Re-armament." July 27, 1954. Mary McLeod Bethune: Building a Better World, Essays and Selected Documents. Ed. Audrey Thomas and Elaine Smith. Indiana University Press, 1999, 58.

Chödrön, Pema. When Things Fall Apart: Heart Advice for Difficult Times. Shambhala Publications, 2002, 85.

Boaler, Jo. "Mistakes Grow Your Brain." youcubed at Stanford University, 2016. www.

youcubed.org/think-it-up/mistakes-grow-brain.

Duckworth, Angela Lee. "Grit: The Power of Passion and Perseverance." TED Talks Education, April 2013. www.ted.com/talks/angela_lee_duckworth_grit_the_power_of_passion_and_perseverance.

Saujani, Reshma. "Teach Girls Bravery, Not Perfection." TED2016, February 2016. www.ted.com/talks/reshma_saujani_teach_girls_bravery_not_perfection?language=en.

WRITES

Shelley, Mary. "Introduction." Frankenstein. H. Colburn and R. Bentley, 1831, ix.

Hansberry, Lorraine. "The Nation Needs Your Gifts: Memo to Negro Youth." Negro Digest, August 1964, 26–29.

"Arianna Huffington: On Redefining Success." www.youtube.com/watch?v=TvbHuE8hbfI.

Rowling, J. K. Very Good Lives. Little, Brown and Company, 2015.

Allende, Isabel. "Commencement Address—San Domenico School." San Domenico School, San Anselmo, California, June 5, 2010. www.isabelallende.com/en/speech/2.

PERMISSIONS

McMillan, Carletta. "Mpumi Lelo Nobiva." Beyond Revealed TV Show, 25 November 2013. https://www.youtube.com/watch?v=MjgNd8AGetw&t=885.

BIBLIOGRAPHY

Svitak, Adora. "What Adults Can Learn from Kids." TED2010, February 2010. www.ted.com/talks/adora_svitak?language=en.

"In order to make anything a reality, you have to dream about it first."

ADORA SVITAK

TEEN POET

ACKNOWLEDGMENTS

Ideas need believers, those special people who have a knack for nudging and nurturing. We're thankful for the support and talents of each person who has helped Quotabelle through the journey of imagining to creating to making the difference we dreamed of from the start.

OUR FAMILIES
Roger Weger • Shawn Weger • Lexi Weger • Parents • Peter • Rosa Frances

UNWAVERING BELIEVERS
Tammy Williams • Dave Kent • Shirley Kappa • Sharon Bertschi • Sally Browne • Emily Williams • Rich Renehan • Beata Renehan • Liz Hamner

ANGELS AND ADVISORS
Donna Morea • Ken Bartee • Sharon Schaaf • Lisa Mascolo • Justin and Deb Dunie • Linda Kent • Bill Tyler • Megan Beyer

EDITORIAL DIRECTOR AT QUARTO PUBLISHING GROUP
Rage Kindelsperger

EARLY THINKERS AND DOERS
Susie Bonvouloir • Meghan Miller Brawley • Rashin Kheiryeh • Chenise Williams • Kathy Lynch • Shelagh Bolger • Jim Gatto • Victoria Cordova • Angela Willard • Kristy Fallica • Steve Meltzer • Sydney Morgan • James Protzman • Alix Nunan • Justin Marcucci • the Nickelfish team • Larry Yanowitch • Lindsay Thomas • Tate Gillman

Cheers,

ALICIA & PAULINE

ABOUT THE AUTHORS

PAULINE WEGER
FOUNDER • CITESEER • STORYTELLER

Pauline is a corporate exec-turned-entrepreneur. As the mom of two daughters, she sees firsthand the importance of spotlighting female role models in creative, modern ways. She has held leadership roles with global corporations, but Pauline's passion for social entrepreneurship was fueled while leading a rebranding initiative for one of the nation's largest food banks. She grew up in a small coastal town just north of Boston and now lives in northern Virginia with her husband and their fur baby, Max, an often-naughty West Highland white terrier.

ALICIA WILLIAMSON
CITESEER • STORYTELLER • EDITOR

Alicia is a wayfaring academic and dedicated wordsmith who loves to use her keyboard for good. A former university educator with a PhD in English, she has researched and taught literature, writing, and women studies. Alicia's passions include archives, activism, outdoors everything, and all kinds of feminism! This northern Minnesota native currently lives in the UK with her husband, baby daughter and their indefatigable border collie.